Johann
STRAUSS

DIE FLEDERMAUS
THE BAT

An Operetta in Three Acts

for Soli, Chorus and Orchestra
with German and English text

VOCAL SCORE

K 06450

JOHANN STRAUSS

DIE FLEDERMAUS
THE BAT

INHALT

INDEX

OUVERTURE.

OVERTURE

Allegretto.

Tempo di valse.

Allegro.

8

Allegro moderato.

10

Tempo di valse.

Nº1.INTRODUCTION.

Allegretto.

Alfred.

PIANO.

(Behind Scenes)
(hinter der Scene)

Täub-chen das entflat-tert ist, stil - le mein Ver-
Dar - ling dove that flew a - way, leav - ing love be-

lan - gen, Täub-chen, das ich oft geküsst,
hind - you, Dove I kissed that hap - py day

lass dich wie - der fan - gen! Täub-chen, hol - des
let my song re-mind you. charm-ing lit - tle

Täub-chen mein, komm, o komm ge-schwin-de; sehnsuchtsvoll ge-denk ich Dein.
dove of mine, come now to your win - dow, full of long-ing I re-pine,

ADELE (spricht über die Wiederholung von Alfred's Gesang): Was ist denn das für ein Gewinsel? Ob man wohl eine Minute nachdenken kann? (eine Münze in ein Papier wickelnd).: Ich muss ihm nur ein Sechserl spendieren, sonst hört der Hofsänger nicht auf!(Wirft das Geld aus dem Fenster.) ....
Was, Rosalinde? Das ist kein Strassentenor, sondern ein Verehrer und nicht einmal von mir, sondern von meiner Gnädigen!(ruft zum Fenster hinaus.):Eine Adele ist hier und keine Rosalinde, wenigstens nicht für Sie! Verlassen Sie den Garten, sonst wird man einen ganz anderen Tenor mit Ihnen singen. -Er verschwindet samt seinem Tenor. Der ist sicher irgendwo einem Männergesangverein ausgekommen. Schade, ich hätt'mir ihn doch näher ansehen sollen;vieleicht kann ich ihn noch erreichen!(Läuft ab)

ROSALINDE(tritt erregt auf). Er ist's!Alfred, er, der mich vor vier Jahren anbetete, als ich noch frei war!Ich habe ihn gleich erkannt an seinem Tenor und an seiner Keckheit. Nur ein Tenor kann so keck sein, und nur ein kecker Mensch kann so Tenor singen!Er wagt es, hier vor dem Hause meines Gatten mich durch sein hohes A zu kompromittieren!

ADELE(eintretend, für sich). Keine Seele mehr zu erblicken. -Ah, da ist meine Gnädige! Jetzt heraus mit der Geschichte; sie sei kurz, aber rührend!(Laut, kläglich.)Gnädige Frau,meine arme Tante ist so krank!

ROSALINDE (fur sich). Sicher hält er mich für treulos, glaubt vielleicht, ich liebe einen anderen, und ich habe doch bloss geheiratet.

ADELE (Kläglicher). Gnädige Frau, meine arme Tante ist krank!

ROSALINDE (immer noch für sich) Aber wie kommt er, der vor vier Jahren spurlos aus Wien verschwand, so plötzlich in diesen Badeort?

ADELE (schluchzend). Gnädige Frau, meine arme Tante ist so krank!

ROSALINDE. Wer ist krank?

ADELE. Meine Tante!

ROSALINDE. Deine Tante?

ADELE. Ja, meine Tante!

ADELE(speaking over the repetition of Alfred's song) What in the world is that whining? Can't one have a moment's peace to think?

I'll have to spend a nickel, or our "Courtsinger" will never stop. (throws the coins out the window) (Alfred stops singing) What, Rosalinda? That is no streetsinger, but an admirer - and not even of mine, but of my mistress'! (calls out the window): Here there's only an Adele, and no Rosalinda, at least not for you.You'd better leave the garden, or you'll be singing a very different tune. ... He disappeared... and his voice, too. He must be an escapee from a Glee Club. Too bad, I should have taken a closer look. Maybe I can still catch him ! (Runs out)

ROSALINDA. (enters, very excited) It is he! Alfred, who adored me so four years ago, when I was still free. I recognized him right away by his voice and by his presumption. Only a tenor could be so presumptuous, and only a presumptuous man sings like a tenor! He dares to come here, right in front of my husband's house, and compromise me with his high " A "!

ADELE (enters, to herself) Not a soul to be seen. -- Ah, there is my mistress! Now, out with my story; make it short, but heartbreaking ! (loud, wailing) Oh, my lady, my poor aunt is so sick!

ROSALINDA(to herself) I'm sure he thinks I am unfaithful, perhaps even in love with some one else, and here I've only gotten married.

ADELE (still more tearfully) My lady, my poor aunt is so sick!

ROSALINDA (still to herself) But why, after disappearing from Vienna without a trace for four years, does he suddenly appear in this resort?

ADELE (sobbing)My lady, my poor aunt is very sick.

ROSALINDA. Who is sick?

ADELE. My aunt.

ROSALINDA. Your aunt?

ADELE. Yes, my aunt.

ROSALINDE. (ungeduldig)Aber kann ich sie denn gesund machen?
ADELE. Das verlange ich gar nicht, wenn Sie es auch könnten.
ROSALINDE. Na also!
ADELE (weiterschluchzend)Aber es ist doch die Pflicht einer guten Nichte, ihre arme Tante zu besuchen und zu fragen:"Wie geht's? Wie befinden Sie sich? Noch immer fidel und munter?"
ROSALINDE. Deine arme, kranke Tante?
ADELE. Darum bitte ich Sie, mir aus Rücksicht für meine nichtige Liebe freien Ausgang zu gewähren.
ROSALINDE. (bestimmt) Unmöglich!
ADELE. (bittend)Gnädige Frau!
ROSALINDE. Unmöglich, sage ich. Hast du denn vergessen, dass mein Gemahl heute seine fünftägige Arreststrafe antreten muss? Dreimal ist sie schon verschoben worden; aber heute muss er sich stellen, sonst wird er gestellt.
ADELE. Aber ich weiss noch immer nicht, warum der gnädige Herr eigentlich eingesperrt wird?
ROSALINDE. Weil er einem Amtsdiener ein paar Hiebe mit der Reitpeitsche gegeben und ihn einen Stockfisch genannt hat.
ADELE. Wegen so einem bisserl?
ROSALINDE. Er hat schon an alle Instanzen appelliert, aber das wird ihm eher schaden als nützen.

ADELE. Wenn es ihm aber dennoch nützt?

ROSALINDE. So wird es dir nichts nützen, denn ich kann dich nicht eine Stunde entbehren.
ADELE. Nicht? O meine arme, arme Tante! So darf ich dich nicht mehr wiedersehen auf Erden? Eine solche Tante wie diese Tante-noch keine Nichte Tante, nannte!...

ROSALINDA (impatiently) Well am I supposed to make her well?
ADELE. I wouldn't ask you to do that, even if you could.
ROSALINDA. Well, then?
ADELE (again sobbing)But it is the duty of a good niece to visit her aunt and to inquire, 'How are you, how do you feel? Still so jolly and bright?"

ROSALINDA. Your poor, sick aunt?
ADELE. So I beg you, in consideration of my dutiful love, let me have the evening off?
ROSALINDA (firmly) Impossible!
ADELE (begging) My lady!
ROSALINDA. I said, impossible! Have you forgotten that my husband has to start his five-day term in prison tonight? It's been postponed three times already; but tonight he has to turn himself in, or they'll drag him in.
ADELE. But I still don't know, why does the Master really have to go to jail?
ROSALINDA. Oh, they caught him duelling again. It started when he called the ambassador a' kraut".

ADELE. What's wrong with that?

ROSALINDA. It was the French ambassador. It wouldn't be so bad, but he kept appealing, until the judge decided to let the prison warden hear his appeals.
ADELE. Maybe if he appeals to the warden, he'll let him free.
ROSALINDA. Well, in any case, you shall not go free this evening; I cannot spare you for one hour.
ADELE. You can't? Oh, my poor, poor aunt! So, I will never be allowed to see you again on this earth? Such an aunt as this one, such an aunt can't be!

Nº 1ª

ROSALINDE (allein). Wie glücklich die alte Tante ist, eine so liebevolle Nichte zu haben! Es wird nicht so gefährlich sein, hoffe ich. Ich kann sie ja nicht entbehren, weil ich nicht allein bleiben darf, wenn mein Mann in der Tat seine Strafe antreten muss. Und der wird er nicht entgehen, denn jetzt hat er die Richter erst recht erbittert gegen sich. (Ihr Blick fällt auf Alfred, der in der Mitteltür erscheint.) Himmel, Alfred!

ALFRED (vortretend). Warum denn nicht: mein Alfred, und mir mit offenen Armen entgegenflogen?

ROSALINDE. Mein Herr, ich bin verheiratet!

ALFRED. Das geniert mich nicht!

ROSALINDE. Aber mich! Entfernen Sie sich!

ALFRED. Ich bin ja nicht gekommen, um mich zu entfernen!

ROSALINDE. Himmel, wenn mein Mann erschiene!

ALFRED. Das geniert mich nicht! Übrigens erscheint er nicht, er muss brummen.

ROSALINDE. Nein, nein! (Den Blick erhebend.) Vater im Himmel, lass ihn nicht brummen, ich bitte dich!

ALFRED. Er muss brummen, da hilft ihm kein Gott!

ROSALINDE. Ich bitte, ich beschwöre Sie, verlieren Sie sich!

ALFRED. Wohlan, ich verliere mich, jedoch nur unter der Bedingung, dass ich wiederkehren darf, wenn Ihr Gemahl brummt. Schwören Sie mir, dass Sie mich empfangen werden, wenn Sie Strohwitwe sind, und ich entferne mich augenblicklich. (Theatralisch.) Schwöre!

ROSALINDE. Es sei .... ich schwöre!

ALFRED. Nun denn...... ich gehe! (Bleibt stehen)

ROSALINDE. (ungeduldig) Sie gehen aber nicht, sondern stehen noch immer! Leben Sie wohl!

ALFRED (singt). Kein Lebewohl! Auf Wiedersehen! Bald bin ich wieder da! (ab).

ROSALINDE (allein). Oh, wenn er nur nicht singen wollte! Seinem Dialog bin ich noch allenfalls gewachsen, aber vor seinem hohen B schmilzt meine Kraft dahin! O Schicksal, Schicksal, warum hast du mir das angetan? In dem Augenblick, wo du mir die Gegenwart des Gatten entziehst, führst du mir das Bild der Vergangenheit vor Augen. Was soll aus der Zukunft meiner Pflichten werden? Meine einzige Hoffnung beruht jetzt noch auf dem Ausspruch des Gerichts. Wird meinem Gatten die Arreststrafe erlassen, dann ist alles gut! Oh, wenn die Richter wüssten, welche Verantwortung sie durch seine Verurteilung auf sich laden, sie würden Gnade walten lassen! (Horcht.) Ha, er kommt! Er zankt mit seinem Advokaten. Ein böses Zeichen!

ROSALINDA (alone). What a happy aunt, to have such a loving niece! I do hope she's not in too much danger. I simply cannot spare her, since I dare not stay here alone while my husband must go to prison. And he has to go now, because he has infuriated the judges so against him. (Her glance falls on Alfred, who appears in the middle door) Good Heaven, Alfred!

ALFRED (advancing). And why not "My Alfred", and fly to me with open arms?

ROSALINDA. Sir, I am a married woman!

ALFRED. I'll overlook that.

ROSALINDA. But I won't! You must say goodbye!

ALFRED. I just got here, why should I say goodbye?

ROSALINDA. Dear Heaven, what if my husband comes in?

ALFRED. I'd overlook that, too. Anyway, he won't come in, he's going to jail.

ROSALINDA. No, no! (raising her eyes) Dear God in Heaven, please don't let him go to jail, I beg of you!

ALFRED. He has to go to jail, God won't help him there.

ROSALINDA. I beg you, I implore you, go, get thee hence!

ALFRED. All right, I shall get me hence -- but on one condition, that I be allowed to return while your husband is behind bars. Promise that you will receive me, during your "legal" separation", and I'll go instantly. (theatrically) Swear it!

ROSALINDA. So be it.... I swear!

ALFRED. Very well.... I go! (stands still)

ROSALINDA. (impatiently) But you're not going at all, you're still standing around. Good-bye!

ALFRED (singing). T'is not goodbye! Soon I shall return! Arrivederci!

ROSALINDA (alone). Oh, if he only would stop singing. His conversation I can resist, but that high "B" just melts my resistance. Oh, Destiny, Destiny, how can you do this to me? In the same instant, you take my husband from me, and you show me this vision from the past. What is to become of my obligations? My only hope is the Judge's decision. If my husband is freed of his prison sentence, all will be well! If the judges only knew what responsibility they take on in declaring a man guilty, they would let mercy prevail! (listens) There, he's coming. He's quarreling with his lawyer. That's a bad sign.

№ 2. TERZETT.

22

25

Andante.

ROSAL.

Ach, mein ar - mer, ar - mer Mann, noch heu - te al - so musst Du
Ah, poor dear, this ver - y day, a - las, you have to go a -

dran? Was kann ich Dir zum Tros - te sa - gen? Wie soll ich das er - tra -
way? How can I bear this sep - a - ra - tion? How give you con - so - la -

rit.

colla parte

Tempo I.

ROSAL.

gen?
-tion?

EISENST.

Ach, mit solchen Ad - vo - ca - ten ist ver - kauft man und ver - ra - then, da ver -
Cur - ses on that aw - ful law - yer, who des-troyed his own em - ploy-er! It's e -

ROSAL.

Und da - ran ist der nur schuld! Sie sind schuld!
And it's all his fault, the cad! You're a cad!

EISENST.

liert man die Ge - duld. Der ist
-nough to drive me mad! And you're

BLIND (tritt wieder ein)

Wer ist schuld?
Who's a cad?

28

30

ROSALINDE (spricht). Also noch verschärft die Strafe? Statt fünf Tage -- acht Tage !

EISENSTEIN. Diese Zulage habe ich Herrn Dr.Stotterbock zu danken.

BLIND. Rei...rei...reizen Sie mich nicht! Sie allein haben durch Ihr Benehmen die Richter erbittert und mich obendrein ko...ko...konfus gemacht. Aber ich will Ihnen nichts nachtragen, und wenn Sie wieder einmal tüchtig eingesperrt werden sollen, vertret ich Sie abermals!

EISENSTEIN. Ja, ich bitte recht sehr !

BLIND. Wenn Sie wieder einmal mit einem Amtsdiener einen Konflikt haben sollten, genieren Sie sich nicht... Das nächste Mal arbeite ich Sie ganz sicher heraus !

EISENSTEIN. Alle Donnerwetter, ich empfehle mich Ihnen !

BLIND. Ihr Diener! (Schnell zur Tür hinaus.)

EISENSTEIN. Ist das ein Vertreter ! Solch blühender Unsinn hat noch in keinem Gerichtssaal gewuchert !

ROSALINDE. Mein armer Gabriel ! Acht lange Tage - und heute noch !

EISENSTEIN. Heute noch !(Singt) Es muss geschieden sein !

ROSALINDE. Und mit so einem Tenor haben sie dich verurteilen können, die Barbaren !

EISENSTEIN. Sie haben mich mit meinem Tenor gleich dort behalten wollen, ich habe verflucht zu Kreuze kriechen müssen, bis man mir noch ein paar Stunden Freiheit bewilligt hat, um mit dir speisen zu können.(Klingelt.)Verdenken kann ich's ihnen nicht : dreimal haben sie mich eingeladen ; wer aber nicht kam, war ich !

ADELE.(mit verweinten Augen, gepresster Stimme). Befehlen ?

EISENSTEIN. Was bedeutet das ?Du hast geweint?Doch nicht um mich, Adele?

ADELE.(schluchzt). Meine arme Tante !

ROSALINDE. Die arme Frau ist sterbenskrank !

EISENSTEIN. Sterbenskrank? Ich habe sie ja soeben hoch zu Esel in die Weinberge reiten sehen.

ADELE.(für sich). O verwünscht !

ROSAL. (blickt auf Adele). So krank ist sie?

ADELE. Wer weiss, ob ihr der Doktor nicht den Esel verordnet hat ?

EISENSTEIN. Eile jetzt in den "Goldenen Löwen" und bestelle ein delikates Souper. Was gut und teuer ist, soll man uns liefern.(Adele will fort.) Noch eins ! Wenn du zurückkehrst, suchst du mir aus meinen alten Kleidern den ältesten, schmutzigsten, zerrissensten und miserabelsten Anzug heraus.

ADELE. Wollen Euer Gnaden betteln gehen?

EISENSTEIN. Nein, aber ich will nicht angebettelt werden in der Gesellschaft, deren Mitglied ich heute nacht sein werde. Vor allem das Souper! Ich will mir heute noch bene tun an meinem Familientische.

ADELE.(meldet im Abgehen). Herr Dr. Falke !

FALKE.(sehr heiter). Ah, da ist er noch !(Küsst Rosalinde die Hand.)Mein Kompliment, schönste aller Frauen! Ich gratuliere von Herzen, dass Sie den Tyrannen auf acht Tage loswerden.(Reicht Eisenstein die Hand.)Aber auch dir wünsche ich Glück, denn die Zugabe von drei Tagen ist immerhin eine Errungenschaft, für die du dem Gerichtshofe eine Dankadresse schuldig bist !

ROSALINDA. Aber Herr Doktor !

ROSALINDA(speaking). So now they have increased your sentence? Instead of five days---eight days!

EISENSTEIN. An increase I owe to the bleating Dr. Blind.

BLIND. D...d...don't prov - voke me. You enraged the j - judges all by yourself and c-c-confused me, as well. But I won't hold it against you, and the next time you go to jail, I'll represent you again in sp - spite of it.

EISENSTEIN. I'm sure you will !

BLIND. If you ever have any more tr - - trouble with that official, don't hesitate... the next time I'm almost sure to get you off.

EISENSTEIN. By God ---- Good-bye!

BLIND. Your servant !(quickly goes out the door)

EISENSTEIN. He calls himself a lawyer ! Such blooming nonsense never grew in any courtyard of law.

ROSALINDA. My poor Gabriel! Eight long days - - and even tonight !

EISENSTEIN. Even this very night.(sings)We have to say Farewell !

ROSALINDA. How could they condemn a tenor? The Barbarians !

EISENSTEIN. They wanted to keep me there, tenor voice and all, this afternoon. I had to beg them for a few hours grace, so I could dine with you. (rings the bell) I can't really blame them ; they "invited" me three times, and I didn't show up.

ADELE.(eyes red with crying, in a sobbing voice.) You rang ?

EISENSTEIN. What's the meaning of this?You've been crying. Surely not because of me, Adele?

ADELE. My poor aunt !

ROSALINDA. The poor woman is deathly ill.

EISENSTEIN. Deathly ill? I just saw her galloping a donkey through the vineyard.

ADELE.(aside) Oh, damn !

ROSALINDA.(looking at Adele). So, that's how sick she is !

ADELE. Who knows, maybe the doctor prescribed the donkey ?

EISENSTEIN. Hurry off now, to the "Golden Lion", and order us a magnificent dinner. Have them send us everything good, and expensive.(Adele starts to go) Another thing ! When you get back, dig out the oldest, dirtiest, most ragged and miserable clothes you can find for me.

ADELE. Is your Lordship going begging ?

EISENSTEIN. No, but I don't want to be begged of by the company I shall be keeping tonight. But first, the dinner ! I shall at least do well by myself at my family table.

ADELE.(announcing as she goes off) Dr. Falke.

FALKE.(delighted). Ah, there he is !(kisses Rosalinda's hand). My compliments, most beautiful of women ! You have my heartfelt congratulations, that for eight days you will be liberated from this tyrant ! (holds his hand out to Eisenstein). But to you also my felicitations ; that increase of three days in prison is an extraordinary accomplishment--- you really should thank your judges !

ROSALINDA. But Dr. Falke !

EISENSTEIN. Lass ihn nur. Wer den Schaden hat, braucht für den Spott nicht zu sorgen! Schicke in den Keller, liebe Frau; die böse Zunge muss genetzt werden, wenn sie nicht zu spitz werden soll.

ROSALINDE. Keine schlechten Witze mehr, lieber Doktor! Wir müssen ja unseren armen Arrestanten ein wenig aufzuheitern suchen. (Ab.)

FALKE. (Rosalinde nachrufend). Freilich, ihn zu zerstreuen und aufzuheitern bin ich ja da, schöne Frau! (Leiser zu Eisenstein). Ich komme, dich zu einem fürstlichen Souper mit den reizenden Koryphäen der Oper einzuladen.

EISENSTEIN. Bist du toll? Ich muss ja binnen einer Stunde meine Strafe antreten.

FALKE. Den Arrest kannst du morgen in aller Frühe antreten. Heute gehst du mit mir in die Villa Orlofskys, des jungen russischen Fürsten, der hier im Bade fabelhafte Summen verschwendet. Damen findest du dort, Damen, sag ich dir, ein wahrer Blütenflor, von der Kamelie bis zum Veilchen!

EISENSTEIN. Sind die Damen etwa die alte Garde der Oper?

FALKE. Wo denkst du hin?(Zungenschnalzend.) Die Elite der ersten Quadrille und dann einige von dem jugendlichen Nachwuchs, die sogenannten Ratten.

EISENSTEIN. Teufel, mir wässert der Mund! Aber der Prinz....

FALKE. .... hat mich dringend ersucht, einige junge Lebemänner meiner Bekanntschaft einzuladen.

EISENSTEIN. Man schmeichelt mir allerdings, dass ich ein liebenswürdiger Gesellschafter bin!

FALKE. Und dabei immer mit den tollsten Einfällen bei der Hand, zum Beispiel vor drei Jahren, als wir den Scheelendorfer Maskenball besuchten...

EISENSTEIN. Ich als Papillon, du als Fledermaus. Haha! Erinnerst du dich noch?

FALKE. (bedeutungsvoll). Oh, so etwas vergisst man nicht so leicht!

EISENSTEIN. Es war ein kapitaler Spass!

FALKE. O ja, für den Papillon, aber nicht für die Fledermaus!

EISENSTEIN. Dr. Häring, der heute präsidierte, war auch dabei. Hielt sich den Bauch vor Lachen und konnte mir nicht oft genug zurufen: "Das ist dir gelungen, Bruder!" - Und heute frug er mich: "Wie heissen Sie?" Und diktierte mir acht Tage. Oh, dieser schlechte gute Freund!(Zieht seine Uhr aus der Tasche, lässt sie repetieren.)

FALKE. Ah, da ist ja der gewisse Rattenfänger!

EISENSTEIN. Was meinst du?

FALKE. Man behauptet, dass du mit dieser niedlichen Repetieruhr alle Kameliendamen köderst, wenn du ihnen den Hof machst. Du versprichst sie einer jeden...

EISENSTEIN. .... aber gegeben habe ich sie noch keiner! (lacht)

FALKE. Spitzbube, du wirst heute nacht abermals diesen Köder auswerfen können, denn ich rechne damit, dass du von der Partie bist?

EISENSTEIN. Oh, let him alone. A wounded man does not worry about a little mockery. Send to the cellar, my darling. The venomous tongue must be dampened, lest it grow too sharp.

ROSALINDA. No more bad jokes, please, dear doctor. We must try to console our poor delinquent.

FALKE. (calling after Rosalinda). Certainly, dear lady -- to console him and to distract him is exactly why I came !(softly to Eisenstein). I came to take you to a princely dinner with an enchanting ballerina from the Opera !

EISENSTEIN. Are you mad? I have to start my prison term in one hour.

FALKE. You can start tomorrow morning, bright and early. Tonight, you will go with me to the Villa of Orlofsky, the young Russian prince, who's been throwing away fabulous sums of money here. Ladies you will find there, ladies, I tell you, a veritable garden in bloom, from camellias to blushing violets!

EISENSTEIN. Are these ladies, perhaps, the old guard of the opera?

FALKE. What do you think? (smacking his lips) The elite of the first Quadrille, and then some of the young new-comers, the little mice, so to say.

EISENSTEIN. The Devil you say, my mouth is watering! But the prince.....

FALKE. .... Has asked me, most urgently, to invite some young playboys of my acquaintance.

EISENSTEIN. Well, I'm flattered that I'm considered such a desirable companion!

FALKE. And always ready with a wild idea... for example, that time three years ago, when we went to the Scheelendorfer Masked Ball...

EISENSTEIN. I as a Butterfly and you as a Bat! You still remember?

FALKE. (meaningfully). It has been difficult to forget!

EISENSTEIN. Oh, that was a capital joke !

FALKE. Oh sure, for the butterfly, but not for the Bat!

EISENSTEIN. Dr. Haring, who presided today, was there, too. He had to hold his stomach from laughing, and he kept telling me "You really pulled a good one, brother." And today he asked me my name and gave me eight days in jail. Oh, these terrible good friends !(takes his watch from his pocket and lets it ring)

FALKE. Ah, there is the famous mouse-trap !

EISENSTEIN. What do you mean?

FALKE. They say you use that charming little clock as bait to court all the, ah, "Ladies of the Camellias". You promise it to each one...

EISENSTEIN. But I still haven't given it to anyone ! (laughs)

FALKE. You rogue, you'll be tossing out this bait again tonight; I'm counting on you, then, to come to the party?

34

Andantino.

Ja, ich glaub, Du hast Recht, die Aus-red' ist nicht schlecht!
I'm con-vinced, you are right, it's on-ly for one night!

Soll Dir das Ge-
What good is your

Soll mir das Ge-fäng-niss nicht schädlich sein, muss
What good is my health in a pri-son cell, I

fäng-niss nicht schädlich sein, ___
health in a pri-son cell,

ich Et-was thun, mich zu zer-streun. Wer kann widerstehn? Ja, ich
might just as well en-joy my-self. How can I re-sist? I'll be

musst Du Et-was thun, Dich zu zer-streun! So kommst Du?
you might just as well en-joy your-self! You'll come then?

bin da-bei!
at your side!

a piacere

Zum Teufel mit Dei-ner Leimsiede
For-get your conscience, let me be your

38

ROSALINDE. (mit einem zerrissenen Rock und alten Hut blickt erstaunt auf die Tanzenden). Was ist denn das?

EISENSTEIN, FALKE (unterbrechen den Tanz).

ROSALINDE. Was treibt ihr denn, meine Herrn?

FALKE. (etwas verlegen). Nicht wahr, das ist mir gelungen?

EISENSTEIN. Er hat mich getröstet.

FALKE. Eine schwierige Aufgabe, aber ich habe sie glücklich gelöst.

EISENSTEIN. Jawohl, ich gehe jetzt in meinen Arrest, als ob ich zu einem Lustgelage ginge!

FALKE. Was bringen Sie uns denn da, gnädige Frau?

ROSALINDE. Die Toilette für unseren Arrestanten. (drückt Eisenstein den Hut auf den Kopf.) Ist dir der Hut recht?

EISENSTEIN (schleudert den Hut fort). Warum nicht gar! Willst du denn einen Räuber aus mir machen?

ROSALINDE. Aber du befahlst ja Adele....

FALKE (nimmt den Rock) Und dieser Kittel! Wenn du den anlegst, lässt dich der Gefängnisdirektor gleich mit 25 bewillkommnen!

ROSALINDE. (erschrocken). Himmel!

FALKE. (greift nach seinem Hute). Gnädige Frau...

ROSALINDE. Sie wollen uns schon verlassen?

FALKE. Es ist schon spät, und ich will dem Gefängnisdirektor, Herrn Frank, seinen neuen Hausgenossen anmelden. Ich werde dich dort erwarten, Freund Eisenstein! (Ab.)

EISENSTEIN. (ruft ihm nach). Meine Empfehlung an die Ratten!

ROSALINDE. An die Ratten?!

EISENSTEIN. Natürlich an die Ratten! Die Ratten illustrieren die Poesie des Kerkers.

ROSALINDE. Gerechter Gott, bei den Ratten wirst du einquartiert!

EISENSTEIN. Warum denn nicht? Es sind ja ganz possierliche Tierchen. Ich werde mich gut mit Ihnen unterhalten. (singt). Juchheissa, hopsassa, trallala!

ROSALINDE. Aber jetzt ist doch nicht Zeit, juchheissa, hopsassa zu singen!

EISENSTEIN. Nein, denn es ist Zeit, an meine Toilette zu denken.

ROSALINDE. Toilette fürs Strafhaus?

EISENSTEIN. Natürlich! Falke meint, es sei leicht möglich, dass ich dort eine geschlossene Gesellschaft finde. (Küsst Rosalinde auf die Stirn.)
    Ich weiss, wie ich mich kleide:
    In schwarzen Samt und Seide
    Mit einem Chapeau bas -
    Gleich bin ich wieder da! (Ab.)

ROSALINDE. (allein). Der Mann ist ja wie ausgewechselt! Mir scheint, er freut sich ordentlich, eingesperrt zu werden. Wenn ich nur wüsste, was ich mit dem da unten anfangen soll? Ich habe geschworen, ihn zu empfangen, und wenn man einmal einen solchen schweren Schwur schwört, muss man diesen Schwur halten, sei es noch so schwer!

ADELE. (bringt auf einer Platte einen Wildschweinkopf mit einem Rosenbukett im Rüssel). Der "Löwe" schickt diesen wilden Schweinskopf.

ROSALINDE. Und du hast das Ungeheuer angenommen?

ADELE. Er hat sonst nichts vorrätig gehabt.

ROSALINDE. (sinnend vor dem Schweinskopf) So muss ich ihn denn annehmen?

ADELE. Freilich, ich habe ihn ja schon bezahlt!

ROSALINDA. (enters with a torn jacket and old hat, looking in astonishment at the dancing). What is all this?

EISENSTEIN, FALKE (interrupt their dance).

ROSALINDA. What are you doing, gentlemen?

FALKE. (a little embarassed) Well, you see I did cheer him up!

EISENSTEIN. Yes, he consoled me.

FALKE. A difficult task, but I managed it.

EISENSTEIN. Yes. I go to jail now as if to an orgy!

FALKE. What's that you've brought us, dear lady?

ROSALINDA. Some feathers for our jailbird! (puts the hat on Eisenstein's head). Is that the proper hat?

EISENSTEIN (flinging the hat away) What's that for? Do you want me to be taken for a thief?

ROSALINDA. But you ordered Adele to....

FALKE. And this dustrag? If you wear that, the warden will lock you up in solitary confinement for twenty years!

ROSALINDA. (frightened) Good heaven!

FALKE. (taking his own hat) My lady...

ROSALINDA. Are you leaving us so soon?

FALKE. It is getting late, and I want to announce his new house-guest to the warden, Herr Frank. I shall be waiting for you there, friend Eisenstein! (exits)

EISENSTEIN. (calling after him) My compliments to the mice!

ROSALINDA. To the mice?

EISENSTEIN. Naturally to the mice. The mice represent the poetry of prison.

ROSALINDA. God in heaven, they'll put you in with the mice?

EISENSTEIN. Why not? Aren't they quite cute little beasts? I shall amuse myself quite well with them. (singing) Yo-heissa, hopsassa, tralala!

ROSALINDA. It seems hardly the time to be singing, yo-heissa, hopsassa!

EISENSTEIN. You're absolutely right. It is time for me to think of dressing!

ROSALINDA. Dressing.... for jail?

EISENSTEIN. Certainly. Falke says it's more than likely I shall meet some of the most exclusive society there. (kisses Rosalinda on the forehead)
    It seems I must be dressed
    To look my very best;
    High hat, black tails, white tie -
    Then quickly, I must fly! (exits)

ROSALINDA. (alone) He's like a different man! He seems delighted to go to prison. If only I knew what to do with the other one! I did promise to receive him, and once one has given one's word, one must keep it, no matter how difficult it is!

ADELE. (brings in a platter with a huge wild boar's head, with a bouquet of roses in it's mouth) The "Lion" sent this boar's head.

ROSALINDA. And you accepted that monster?

ADELE. It was all they had.

ROSALINDA. (meditating) So I must accept him?

ADELE. Certainly, I've already paid for him!

ROSALINDE. (ohne auf Adele zu achten). Meinen Schwur muss ich halten. Empfangen werde ich ihn, aber nur, um ihn gleich wieder zu entlassen. Aber Adele muss ich mir aus dem Wege schaffen. (Laut zu Adele.) Nun, wie befindet sich denn deine alte kranke Tante nach der Eselspartie?'

ADELE. I nu..... so so! Den Umständen angemessen......

ROSALINDE. Sollte diese alte kranke Tante nicht ein junger, gesunder Vetter sein?

ADELE. Gnädige Frau, ich bitte recht sehr....

ROSALINDE. Aber gleichviel, Tante oder Vetter, ich gebe dir den Urlaub ohne Fragezeichen.

ADELE. Wahrhaftig, gnädige Frau? Aber früher haben Sie mir ihn rundweg abgeschlagen?

ROSALINDE. Weil ich früher verdriesslich war, jetzt bin ich bei besserer Laune.

ADELE. Weil der gnädige Herr eingesperrt wird?

ROSALINDE. Mamsell Naseweis!

ADELE. Bitte um Verzeihung, gnädige Frau!

EISENSTEIN. (in eleganter Balltoilette, parfümiert sich). So: die Haare Violet de Mars, die Wäsche Fleur d'Orange! Jetzt habe ich nur noch den Frack zu wässern mit Eau de Cologne. Hast du nicht gehört, Adele? Eau de Cologne habe ich befohlen.

ADELE. (holt einen Flakon).

EISENSTEIN. (sich bespritzend). So, jetzt dufte ich anständig!

ROSALINDE. Und diese strenge Balltoilette hast du für die Gefangenen gemacht?

EISENSTEIN. Damit sie sehen, dass ich ihrer würdig bin! Diese Herren Spitzbuben pflegen uns gleich über die Achsel anzuschauen. Habt ihr nicht eine Rose, Kamelie oder...(bemerkt das Bukett im Rüssel des Schweinkopfes) erlauben schon, Baron Wildschwein! (Befestigt die Rosen in seinem Knopfloch).

ROSALINDE. Unbegreiflich!

EISENSTEIN. Aber es ist Zeit. Leb wohl!

ROSALINDE. Wie? Ohne zu soupieren?

EISENSTEIN. Ich werde mit den Ratten soupieren.

ADELE. Und was geschieht mit dem Schweinskopf?

ROSALINDE. Bring ihn deiner armen kranken Tante!

ADELE. Tausend Dank, gnädige Frau! Das wird die arme Frau mit dem schwachen Magen recht erquicken!

EISENSTEIN. (affektiert die Arme ausbreitend). Rosalinde, meine teure Rosalinde!

ROSALINDE. (bewegt in seine Arme stürzend). Mein armer Gabriel!

EISENSTEIN. Süsse Träume mögen dich umgaukeln, während ich die ganze Nacht ruhelos durchwachen werde. (macht Tanzschritte.)

ADELE. (seufzt). Wie traurig!

EISENSTEIN. In solcher Situation hat man nur die Wahl, entweder in Schmerz zu vergehen oder sich rasch voneinander loszureissen. Reissen wir uns los!

ROSALINDE. (schluchzt). Unmöglich!

ADELE. Probieren Sie es nur; vielleicht geht's doch!

EISENSTEIN. Ermanne dich, Weib, ermanne dich!

ROSALINDA. (without noticing Adele) I must keep my word. I will receive him - and then I will dismiss him immediately! But first I must get Adele out of the way. (loud, to Adele) Ah, how is your sick old aunt feeling after her donkey excursion?

ADELE. Well, er... so, so. Under the circumstances,..

ROSALINDA. This sick old aunt couldn't be a healthy young cousin, could it?

ADELE. My lady, I beg you....

ROSALINDA. No matter, aunt or cousin - I give you the evening free, and no questions asked.

ADELE. Do you mean it, my lady? But before you absolutely refused!

ROSALINDA. Well, I was in a bad mood before, but I'm feeling better now.

ADELE. Since the master is going to jail?

ROSALINDA. Little Miss Busybody?

ADELE. I beg your pardon, my lady!

EISENSTEIN. (in elegant evening attire, perfuming himself) So: for the hair, Violet de Mars, for the handkerchief, Fleur d'Orange. Now I have only to water the tails with Eau de Cologne! Did you hear me, Adele? I called for Eau de Cologne!

ADELE. (brings a flacon).

EISENSTEIN. (sprays himself liberally) There, now I smell presentable.

ROSALINDA. And this elegant evening attire is for the benefit of your fellow prisoners?

EISENSTEIN. So they see I am worthy to join them! Those rogues shall not look down their noses at us! Have you a rose, or a camellia, or.... (noticing the bouquet in the wild boar's mouth) with your permission, milord Hamlet! (fastens the flower in his lapel)

ROSALINDA. I don't believe it!

EISENSTEIN. The time has come! Farewell!

ROSALINDA. What? Without the dinner?

EISENSTEIN. I shall dine with the mice!

ADELE. But what will become of the wild boar's head?

ROSALINDA. Take it to your poor sick old aunt.

ADELE. Oh, a thousand thanks, my lady! This will make her very happy--the poor old woman has such a weak stomach!

EISENSTEIN. (affectedly throwing his arms open) Rosalinda, my darling Rosalinda!

ROSALINDA. (throwing herself into his arms, with great emotion) My poor Gabriel!

EISENSTEIN. May sweet dreams enchant you, while I am spending a restless, wakeful night! (dances a few steps)

ADELE. How sad! (sighing)

EISENSTEIN. In such a situation, one must choose to die of pain, or to tear oneself away quickly. We must tear ourselves away!

ROSALINDA. (sobbing) Impossible!

ADELE. You ought to try, at least. You might be able to!

EISENSTEIN. Pull yourselves together, women, pull yourselves together.

No. 4. TRIO
Nº 4. TERZETT.

44

ROSALINDE.(allein). Er weint und tanzt zugleich. Wie leichtsinnig doch diese Männer sind! Er wird sich schnell zu trösten wissen, während ich arme Frau einsam und verlassen um ihn traure, bis..... der andere kommt! Nein, der andere darf nicht kommen; ich gehe hinunter und lasse alle Türen schliessen.(Geht gegen die Tür.) Ja, ich sperre zu! (Kehrt langsam wieder um.) Ich kann nicht, ich darf aber auch nicht! Ich habe geschworen, und was man geschworen hat, muss man halten, sonst ist man verloren.(Horcht gegen die Tür.) Man kommt: er ist's! (Setzt sich.) Er wird mich trösten wollen, da wird er sich aber irren. Ich bleibe untröstlich!

ALFRED. (in der Tür). Er brummt!

ROSALINDE. (mit einem Seufzer) Er brummt!

ALFRED. (bemerkt den Wein auf dem Tisch). Sie haben wie ich sehe, schon dafür gesorgt, mich gastlich zu empfangen. Danke für die freundliche Auf - merksamkeit! (Füllt ein Glas.)

ROSALINDE. (pikiert). Machen Sie keine Umstände, bitte!

ALFRED. Sie haben recht. Da sind ja auch die Attribute des legitimen Hausherrn : Schlafrock und Kappe! Wohlan, ich will mich auf einen Augenblick in mein verlorenes Paradies zurückträumen. Ich will mir einbilden, Ihr Gemahl zu sein. (Zieht seinen Rock aus und bekleidet sich mit Schlafrock und Kappe!)

ROSALINDE. Mein Gott, was tun Sie denn?

ALFRED. Kommod mach ich mir's! (Isst und trinkt.) Hast du keinen Appetit, liebes Weibchen?

ROSALINDE. Das ist doch zu arg!

ALFRED. Morgen früh keinen Kaffee, liebe Alte! Ich bitte um ein russisches Frühstück : Kaviar, Roastbeef, Heringssalat.....

ROSALINDE. Zum Frühstück! Er wird doch nicht....

ALFRED. Und Rostopschin... ich liebe starke Getränke!

ROSALINDE.(mit aufgehobenen Händen). Ich bitte, ich beschwöre Sie, verlassen Sie mich jetzt! Ich habe Sie empfangen, um meinen Schwur zu halten. Doch nun genug! Sie werden durch Fortsetzung dieses Scherzes nicht diejenige kompromittieren wollen, die Ihnen einst teuer war.

ALFRED. Kompromittieren will ich Sie nicht, aber Ihren Wein will ich auch nicht stehen lassen. Also trinken wir (einschenkend) und singen wir dazu!

ROSALINDE. Nein, nicht singen; nur nicht singen!!

ALFRED. Ei, warum denn nicht? Sie haben doch einst meinen Tenor so gern gehört!

ROSALINDE. Ach, das ist's ja eben! Nur zu gerne!

ALFRED. (schenkt ein und trinkt). Frisch gesungen!

ROSALINDA. (alone). He cries and dances at the same time. How giddy men are! He will be consoled soon enough, while I, poor woman, shall mourn for him, all alone and abandoned, until....... until the other one arrives! No, the other must must not arrive! I'll go lock all the doors. (Goes toward the door) Yes, I'll lock them! (turns slowly back) I cannot, and I should not. I gave my word, and if one gives one's word, one must keep it, or surely one is lost. (listens toward the door) Some one's coming; It's he! (sits down) He'll try to console me, but he's very mistaken there. I shall remain unconsoled.

ALFRED.(in the door) He's gone to jail?

ROSALINDA.(with a sigh) He's gone to jail!

ALFRED. (noticing the wine on the table) I see you have already prepared to receive me with the proper hospitality. Thank you, for your, er,.... thoughtfulness! (fills a glass)

ROSALINDA. (piqued) Do make yourself at home!

ALFRED. You are right. Here are the accouterments of the master of the house; dressing-gown and nightcap! Well, in a moment I shall be dreaming myself back into my lost paradise! I shall pretend I am your husband! (takes off his coat and puts on the dressing-gown and cap).

ROSALINDA. Good Lord, what are you doing?

ALFRED. Making myself comfortable.(eats and drinks) Have you no appetite, my little wifey?

ROSALINDA. That's too much!

ALFRED. No coffee in the morning, old girl. I'd think I'll have a Russian breakfast: caviar, stroganoff, blinchiki....

ROSALINDA. For breakfast?! He's not planning to...

ALFRED. And vodka, of course... I am fond of the straight alcohol.

ROSALINDA.(lifting her hands) I beg you, I implore you, leave me now. I received you, to keep my word. Now it's enough! You wouldn't want to compromise one whom you once held so dear, with this little joke!

ALFRED. I certainly do not want to compromise you - but I also do not want to leave your wine un - tasted. So come, let us drink(pours some wine) and let us sing!

ROSALINDA. No, no singing! Just don't sing!!

ALFRED. Why not? You used to be rather fond of my singing!

ROSALINDA. Exactly! Too fond!

ALFRED. (pours and drinks a glass) Let us sing anew!

№ 5. FINALE.

(a) Trinklied. b) Couplets. c) Terzett.)

Rosalinde.
Alfred.

PIANO.

Allegretto moderato.

ALFRED.

Trin- ke, Liebchen, trinke schnell;
Drink, my darling, come what may,

trin- ken macht die Au-gen hell; sind die schö-nen Äuglein klar, siehst du Al-les
wine will chase the clouds a-way. When your love-ly eyes are clear, all your doubts will

un poco meno mosso.

licht und wahr; siehst, wie heisse Lieb ein Traum, der uns äff't sehr, siehst, wie ew'ge
dis-ap-pear; you will see true, love's a dream, mak-ing fools of us; faith-ful-ness, a

Tempo I.

Treue Schaum; so 'was giebt's nicht mehr! Flieht auch manche Il-lu-sion,
foolish scheme; why make such a fuss? All il-lu-sion proves in vain,

rit.

die Dir einst Dein Herz er-freut, giebt der Wein Dir Tröstung schon durch Ver-ges-sen-
love's young dream becomes re-gret, Have some wine to ease the pain, help you to for-

nicht zu än-dern ist!
-call the joys we've known!

nicht zu än-dern ist!
-call the joys we've known!

colla parte *a tempo*

MARZIALE

ROSALINDE(spricht:)Ich höre Stimmen;man spricht unten! Weh mir!(zu Alfred) Hören sie,man kommt die
ROSALINDE(speaks:) I hear voices; someone's talking below! Good Heaven!(to Alfred)Listen, someone's coming

Treppe herauf! ALFRED:Das genirt mich nicht! ROS.:Himmel welche Lage!
up the stairs! ALFRED:I'll overlook everything!ROS.:Heaven, what a situation!

FRANK(öffnet die Thür und
    spricht draussen):
FRANK(opens the door and
    speaks, offstage):
Bleibt nur noch vorläufig...
    Wait for me.......

draussen,(tritt ein) Erschrecken Sie nicht, gnadige Frau,ich bin Gefangnissdirector Frank und kann....
outside(enters) Do not be alarmed,dear lady,I am prison-director Frank.........................

mir das Vergnügen nicht versagen,Ihren renitenten Herrn Gemahl persönlich
in sein Stillleben zu geleiten.
and I could not deny myself the pleasure of offering your somewhat reluctant
husband my personal escort to his new bar-room - ah, prison, that is.

ROSALINDE(verwirrt)
Aber mein Gemahl ist ja..
ROSALINDE(confused)But
my husband is already...

ROS.:So schweigen Sie doch, 55
wir sind nicht allein!
ROS.:Will you be still?
We are not alone!

c) TERZETT.

Allegro non troppo.

FRANK.

nein, ich zweif-le gar nicht mehr, doch da ich fort nun muss. so
no, my mind is quite at ease, all doubt I shall dis-miss. It's

ROSAL.

Den Ab - schieds -
The fare - well

ge - ben Sie, ich bit - te sehr, sich schnell den Ab - schiedskuss!
get - ting late, so if you please, give him the fare - well kiss!

cresc.

riten. a piacere

kuss? Nun denn, wenn es sein muss, da ha-ben Sie den
kiss? Well, then, since you in-sist, I guess I will be

ALFR.

Den Ab-schiedskuss!
The fare-well kiss!

Den Abschiedskuss!
The fare-well kiss!

fz

Vivace con fuoco.   Tempo I.

ALFRED.

Kuss!   Soll ich schon brummen mussen fur Ihren werthen Herrn Ge-
kissed!   To pri-son you dis-miss me to take your worthy hus-band's

poco rit.

Allegretto.

Ach, schonen Sie mich! Ach!
He must not find out! Ah!

- lich! Ganz si - cher - lich!
- surd! How can you doubt!

(Frank zuruckkehrend) Fol-gen Sie nun schnell, der Wagen ist zur
(Frank returns) Quick-ly let us go, my carriage waits be-

Allegretto.

FRANK.

Stell, drum fort, drum fort, nur schnell. Mein schönes, grosses Vo-gel-haus, es
- low; come on, come on, let's go. My a-vi-a-ry's ve-ry grand, it's

ist ganz na-he hier. Viel Vö-gel flattern ein und aus, be-kommen frei Quar-
ai-ry as can be. The birds that fly there, by com-mand, re-ceive their lod-ging

tier. Drum lad' ich Sie ganz höf-lich ein, Ver-ehr-te-ster, ich bitt', dort
free. You are in-vit-ed, sir, to be, I hope, my hon-oured guest. We

cresc.

64

L'istesso tempo.

Ende des ersten Akt
End of first Act

SECOND ACT
Zweiter Akt.

No. 6 ENTREACT und CHOR.
Grosser Gartensalon und Garten in der Villa Orlofsky, glänzend beleuchtet. Melanie, Faustine, Felicitas, Sidi, Minni, Hermine, Sabine, Natalie. Weitere Ballerinen, Ali Bey, Ramusin, Murray, Carikoni. Herren.

No. 6 ENT'ACTE AND CHORUS
A great salon and garden in the Villa Orlofsky, brilliantly lit up. Melanie, Faustine, Felicitas, Sidi, Minni, Hermine, Sabine, Natalie, other ballet dancers, Ali Bey, Ramusin, Murray, Carikoni and gentlemen.

72

Beim Abgang des Chores wird der Schluss vom Zeichen O wiederholt.
As the Chorus exits, the exit should be repeated from the sign ⊕

MELANIE. (spricht) Das muss man sagen, diese Villa Orlofsky ist ein wahres Paradies!

FAUSTINE. Eine Oase in der Sandwüste dieses Badeorts!

ALI BEY. Ganz recht, eine Oase in der Wüste! Wir Ägypter kennen das!

FELICITAS. Aber wo ist denn eigentlich unser splendider Wirt, der Prinz?

SIDI. Ich bin schon sehr neugierig, ihn kennenzulernen. Er hätte uns doch eigentlich empfangen sollen.

RAMUSIN. Das tut er nie! Er lässt seine Gäste gern erst ein wenig warm werden. Der Empfang langweilt ihn.

MURRAY. Wir in Kanada werden nicht so leicht warm!

ALI BEY. Die russische Heizung ist aber nicht schlecht!

CARIKONI. Übrigens ist es noch früh, kaum zehn Uhr.

MELANIE. Wir sind noch nicht einmal alle beisammen.

FAUSTINE. Dr. Falke, der die Arrangements übernahm, hat uns für heute ganz besondere Überraschungen versprochen.

FELICITAS. Er selbst ist aber noch nicht da.

CARIKONI. Ich mache der Gesellschaft einen Vorschlag. Folgen Sie mir ins Spielzimmer, ich lege ein Bänkchen.

FAUSTINE. (zu Murray) Ich habe mein Portemonnaie vergessen. Werden Sie mir das Ihre leihen?

MURRAY. Bedaure, wir in Kanada verlieren unser Geld am liebsten selbst!

MINNI. (zu Ramusin) Was Sie gewinnen, gehört mir?

RAMUSIN. Und was ich verliere?

CARIKONI. Das gehört mir!

ALLE. (singen) Wie fliehen schnell die Stunden fort,
Die Zeit wird sicher keinem lang,
Es heisst ja hier das Losungswort:
Amüs'ment, Amüs'ment! (gehen ab.)

IDA. ADELE, sehr elegant gekleidet.

IDA. (erregt) In der Tat, ich kann nicht genug staunen dich hier zu finden!

ADELA. (ebenso) Und ich kann nicht genug staunen über dein Erstaunen.

IDA. Hast du denn einen Freund hier?

ADELE. Noch nicht; aber wenn ich ihn hier finden wollte, brauchte ich nicht lange zu suchen.

IDA. Aber um Himmels willen, sag mir nur, wer dich eingeladen hat?

ADELE. Wer? Mir scheint, mein Schwesterchen will sich lustig machen über mich. Oder sollte es den Brief an mich im Schlaf geschrieben haben?

IDA. Ich - ich hätte an dich geschrieben?

ADELE. Mit der dringenden Bitte, mich frei zu machen in grosser Toilette in der Villa Orlofsky zu erscheinen.

IDA. Das hätte ich dir geschrieben?

ADELE. Oder der grösseren Deutlichkeit wegen schreiben lassen.

IDA. Ich weiss von nichts. Sicher hat sich jemand einen Spass gemacht.

ADELE. Wehe dann dem Spassvogel! Ich lasse unsere alte Tante sterbenskrank werden, lasse ihr erst einen Esel, dann einen Schweinskopf verschreiben, bade mich in Tränenfluten, bis ich einen Ausgang erjammere, mache heimlich eine Zwangsanleihe aus der Garderobe meiner Gnädigen, schwebe reizend wie eine Feenkönigin daher und werde von meiner Schwester empfangen, als ob ich fünf Gulden von ihr ausleihen wollte. Aber so tief sind wir noch nicht gesunken, Gott sei Dank!

IDA. Aber ich bitte dich! Bedenke nur selbst, du... ein Stubenmädchen in unserer Gesellschaft!

MELANIE. You must admit, this Villa Orlofsky is a real Paradise!

FAUSTINE. An oasis in the sands of this seaside resort!

ALI BEY. Precisely, an oasis in the desert! We Egyptians understand that!

FELICITAS. But where is our splendid host, the prince?

SIDI. I am awfully curious to meet him. He really should have greeted us.

RAMUSIN. He never does that. He lets his guests warm up first. Greeting them bores him.

MURRAY. In Canada, we don't warm up so quickly.

ALI BEY. The Russians seem to have better heating systems.

CARIK. Anyway, it's early still - not even ten o'clock.

MELANIE. Everyone's not even here yet.

FAUSTINE. Dr. Falke, who's in charge of the arrangements, promised some special surprises for tonight.

FELICITAS. He's not even here, himself.

CARIKONI. I'll make you a business proposition: come into the gambling room, and I'll make your fortune! I'll be the banker.

FAUSTINE. (to Murray) Oh, I seem to have forgotten my purse. Will you lend me your wallet?

MURRAY. Sorry, but we Canadians like to lose our own money!

MINNI. (to Ramusin) Whatever you win is mine?

RAMUSIN. And what I lose?

CARIKONI. That is mine!

ALL. (sing): How quickly happy hours are passed,
The time tonight is flying fast;
The joys that royalty commands
Are champagne, song and dance.

IDA and Adele appear, very fashionably dressed.

IDA (very excited) I just can't get over my surprise at finding you here!

ADELE. (equally so) And I can't get over your surprise.

IDA. Have you got a friend here?

ADELE. Not yet, but I'm sure I could find one soon enough, if I wanted to.

IDA. For Heaven's sake, tell me who invited you?

ADELE. Who? It seems my little sister is teasing me! Or maybe you wrote that letter in your sleep?

IDA. I? I wrote a letter to you?

ADELE. Yes, absolutely begging me to get the evening off, get myself all dressed up and come to the Orlofsky Villa.

IDA. I wrote that to you?

ADELE. Unless you had someone else write it, to make it legible.

IDA. I don't know a thing about it. Someone's playing a joke on you.

ADELE. Woe to the Joker! I've made our old aunt deathly ill, given her donkey rides and wild boar's heads, and bathed myself in tears to boot, just to get the evening off. I've raided my lady's wardrobe, and come flying here like the fairy queen, to be greeted by my own sister as if I wanted to borrow a nickel! Thank Heaven I haven't sunk that low yet!

IDA. Please! What are you thinking of -- a chambermaid, in such society!

74

ADELE. Nun, gar zu viel darfst du dich nicht mit deiner Charge brüsten, solange du noch im letzten Glied des Korps der Rache figurierst!

IDA. Bitte recht sehr; Zweite Quadrille, erste Figur!

ADELE. Alle Hochachtung!

IDA. Indes, du siehst nicht übel aus.... da bist du einmal.... niemand kennt dich hier. Ich will es wagen, dich als Künstlerin vorzustellen.

ADELE. Als Künstlerin? Nun, vielleicht akzeptiert man mich dafür.

IDA. Man kommt! Spiel deine Rolle gut, sonst blamiertst du mich und dich!

ADELE. Ich werde mir alle Mühe geben.

ORLOFSKY. (eine Zigarette rauchend) Ich habe in meinen achtzehn Jahren vierzig durchlebt, Doktor. Alles langweilt mich; ich kann nicht mehr lachen. (seufzt) Meine Millionen sind mein Unglück!

FALKE. Das Unglück will ich gern mit Ihnen teilen, Durchlaucht!

ORLOFSKY. Und meinen Sie, dass wir heute lachen werden?

FALKE. Ich hoffe es, Durchlaucht. Sie haben mir plein pouvoir gegeben, und ich war bemüht, einen kleinen dramatischen Scherz vorzubereiten.

ORLOFSKY. Wie heisst das Stück?

FALKE. Rache einer Fledermaus!

ORLOFSKY. Der Titel ist originell genug!

IDA. (leise zu Adele) Der Junge ist der Prinz.

ADELE. Noch so klein und schon Prinz?

FALKE. (bemerkt Adele, für sich) Da ist sie; mein Briefchen hat gewirkt. (Zum Prinzen, auf Adele deutend) Das ist schon eine meiner handelnden Personen.

ORLOFSKY. (fixiert Adele durchs Lorgnon) Wahrscheinlich die Soubrette?

IDA. (vorstellend) Fräulein Olga, mein Fräulein Schwester Olga, Durchlaucht.

ORLOFSKY. Olga? Das ist ein Name aus meinem Kalender. (zu Adele) Sprechen Sie russisch?

ADELE. Nein, das ist mir zu kalt.

ORLOFSKY. Natürlich auch Künstlerin?

IDA. Und was für eine! Ich sage nichts als theaterakademische Spezialität!

ORLOFSKY. Das lasse ich mir gefallen! Ich liebe die Künstlerinnen, besonders die angehenden. Sind Sie also eine angehende?

ADELE. Man hat wenigstens schon öfters bei meinen Leistungen gesagt: Es geht an!"
(Lachen hinter der Szene)

FALKE. Ah, unsere Gesellschaft unterhält sich schon beim Spiel. Sicher ist Carikoni der Verführer. Wollen Durchlaucht nicht teilnehmen?

ORLOFSKY. Nein, ich könnte zufällig gewinnen, und das langweilt mich. Aber Sie, meine Damen, hätten vielleicht die Güte, ein paar tausend Francs für mich zu wagen? (Adele eine Brieftasche reichend) Wollen Sie mit dem Inhalt dieser Brieftasche mein Glück auf die Probe stellen?

ADELE. Mit Vergnügen! Aber wenn wir Unglück haben sollten?

ORLOFSKY. So werde ich das Glück haben, Sie bald wieder hier zu sehen.

IDA. (abgehend zu Adele) Wie gefällt dir der Russe?

ADELE. Er amüsiert mich mit seiner Langeweile.
(beide ab.)

ADELE. Well, I can't see you have so much to brag about, dancing in the last row!

IDA. I beg your pardon! Second Quadrille, first figure!

ADELE. My compliments!

IDA. I must admit, you don't look so bad... and you did get in.... nobody here knows you. I'll try it -- I'll present you as an actress.

ADELE. As an actress? Well, they might accept me for that.

IDA. Some one's coming! Play your part well, or we'll both be lost!

ADELE. I'll give it all I've got! Do my best!

ORLOFSKY. (smoking a cigarette) In the eighteen years of my life, I seem to have lived forty, Doctor. Everything bores me. I am unable to laugh. (sighing) My millions are my misfortune.

FALKE. Your misfortune is one I'd gladly share, your Highness!

ORLOFSKY. So you really believe we shall laugh this evening?

FALKE. I hope so, your Highness. You gave me a free hand, and I have planned for a rather dramatic little comedy.

ORLOFSKY. What's the title of your play?

FALKE. The vengeance of a Bat!

ORLOFSKY. The title is sufficiently original!

IDA. (softly to Adele) The young one is the prince.

ADELE. So young, and already a prince?

FALKE. (noticing Adele, to himself) There she is; my little note worked. (to the prince, indicating Adele) There is a member of my cast of characters already.

ORLOFSKY. (regarding Adele through his lorgnon) The soubrette, I presume?

IDA. (introducing) Miss Olga, my sister Olga, your Highness!

ORLOFSKY. Olga? That is the name of my wolfhound! (to Adele) Do you speak Russian?

ADELE. Only when I'm in a hurry.

ORLOFSKY. You are, of course, an actress also?

IDA. And what an actress! I need hardly mention her theatrical accomplishments.

ORLOFSKY. Allow me to imagine them. I adore actresses, especially the rising young talents. Are you one of those?

ADELE. People have often said of my performances, "How true to life"
(laughter behind scenes)

FALKE. Ah, already our guests are amusing themselves with gambling. I'm sure Carikoni is the seducer. Would your Highness care to join them?

ORLOFSKY. No, I might win, and that is so boring. But you, dear ladies, would perhaps do me the favor of risking a few thousand? (hands Adele a wallet) Would you try my luck with the contents of this?

ADELE. With pleasure! But what if we are unlucky?

ORLOFSKY. Then I shall have the good luck of seeing you soon again!

IDA. (leaving with Adele) How do you like the Russian?

ADELE. He amuses me very much with his boredom!
(exit both)

ORLOFSKY. Nun erklären Sie mir doch, Doktor, was Sie vorhaben?
FALKE. Gönnen mir Durchlaucht das Vergnügen der Überraschung. Vorläufig nur das eine: diese Olga ist die Kammerjungfer unseres Helden.
IVAN. (meldet). Der Marquis von Renard!
FALKE. Das ist unser Held selbst!
EISENSTEIN. (tritt ein). Ah, da bist du ja! Du siehst, ich habe mich beeilt. Das Souper hat doch noch nicht begonnen?
FALKE. O nein.
EISENSTEIN. Und die Damen, die reizenden Damen, die du mir versprochen hast?
FALKE. Sind alle hier im Speisezimmer versammelt.
EISENSTEIN. (mit einem Schritt nach rechts) Hier?
ORLOFSKY. (ihm entgegen). Sie wollen die Güte haben, mit uns zu soupieren, mein Herr? Ich heisse Sie willkommen.
EISENSTEIN. (verbeugt sich, dann leise zu Falke) Wer ist denn das junge hübsche Bürschchen?
FALKE. (vorstellend) Prinz Alexander Orlofsky, unser Gastgeber.
EISENSTEIN. Das... das wäre....
ORLOFSKY. Woher dies Staunen?
EISENSTEIN. Verzeihen Durchlaucht, aber die Tscherkessen, die ich bis jetzt kennenlernte, waren sämtliche grösser und umfangreicher.
FALKE. (leise zu Orlofsky) Ich habe eine göttliche Idee. Ich lade seine Frau ein.
ORLOFSKY. Sie wird nicht kommen.
FALKE. Sie kommt! Ich habe ein Mittel. Beschäftigen Sie nur einen Augenblick den Mann. (Im folgenden schreibt Falke einen Brief und lässt ihn durch einen Diener expedieren)
ORLOFSKY. (sehr ernst zu Eisenstein) Eine Frage, Herr Marquis.
EISENSTEIN. Bitte, bitte.....
ORLOFSKY. Ich ersuche Sie als Mann von Ehre zu antworten - aufrichtig - offenherzig - ohne Rückhalt!
EISENSTEIN. Wa.... was?...
ORLOFSKY. Trinken Sie ein Gläschen Madeira mit mir?
EISENSTEIN. Und das ist alles?
ORLOFSKY. (ungeduldig) Trinken Sie!?
EISENSTEIN. Mit dem grössten Vergnügen!
ORLOFSKY. (ruft) Madeira, Ivan!
EISENSTEIN. (für sich) Und zu dieser Frage eine Einleitung, als ob der durchlauchtigste Grünschnabel mein Beichtvater wäre!
ORLOFSKY. Setzen Sie sich. - Nun, so setzen Sie sich doch!
EISENSTEIN (fällt in einen Sessel) Ich sitze schon!

ORLOFSKY, EISENSTEIN, FALKE, IVAN
mit Wein und Gläsern

ORLOFSKY. Trinken Sie!
EISENSTEIN. Zu dienen! (Schenkt sich hastig ein, für sich) Wie der mit mir herumkommandiert!
ORLOFSKY. Hören Sie mich an! Ich muss Sie vor allen Dingen mit meinen nationalen Eigentümlichkeiten bekannt machen.

ORLOFSKY. Now, Doctor, kindly enlighten me as to your intentions.
FALKE. Allow me the pleasure of the surprise, your Highness. So far, only one small fact: our friend Olga is the chambermaid of our hero!
IVAN. (announcing) The Marquis de Renard!
FALKE. That is our hero himself!
EISENSTEIN. (enters) Ah, there you are! You see, I came as quickly as I could. The Dinner has not yet begun?
FALKE. Oh, no.
EISENSTEIN. And the ladies, the charming ladies you promised me?
FALKE. They are all here, in the dining room.
EISENSTEIN. (taking a step to the right) There?
ORLOFSKY. (going to meet him) Are you going to do us the honor of supping with us, Marquis? Allow me to welcome you.
EISENSTEIN. (bows, then softly to Falke) Who's the little boy?
FALKE. (introducing them) Prince Alexander Orlofsky, our host.
EISENSTEIN. He..... he's the.....
ORLOFSKY. What surprises you?
EISENSTEIN. Forgive me, your Highness, but the Russians I've met before were much larger and, er.... voluminous.
FALKE. (softly to Orlofsky) I have a marvellous idea. I'll invite his wife.
ORLOFSKY. She will not come.
FALKE. Oh, yes she will. I have a way. Please, you keep the husband busy a moment. (Falke writes a letter during the following, and sends it by a servant).
ORLOFSKY. (very earnestly to Eisenstein) One question, Marquis.
EISENSTEIN. By all means!
ORLOFSKY. I beg of you to answer as a man of honour ---- sincerely --- openheartedly ---- unreservedly.
EISENSTEIN. Wha..... what?....
ORLOFSKY. Will you drink a glass of Madeira with me?
EISENSTEIN. That is all?
ORLOFSKY. (impatient) Will you drink?
EISENSTEIN. With the greatest of pleasure!
ORLOFSKY. (calls) Ivan, Madeira!
EISENSTEIN. (to himself) And for that, an introduction as if his greenhorn Highness were my confessor. Russians!
ORLOFSKY. Be seated. I said, be seated!

EISENSTEIN. (falls into a chair) I am seated already!

ORLOFSKY, EISENSTEIN, FALKE, IVAN
with wine and glasses

ORLOFSKY. Drink!
EISENSTEIN. At your service! (hastily pouring a glass, to himself) He certainly orders me around!
ORLOFSKY. Now listen to what I say. There are certain of my national peculiarities with which you should be acquainted.

№ 7. COUPLETS.

EISENSTEIN(spricht - zwischen den ersten und zweiten couplet von No. 7). Gehorsamer Diener! Ein echt russisches, drastisches Mittel! Wenn jeder, der sich langweilt, hinausgeworfen wird, werden sich sicher alle Gäste amusieren!

EISENSTEIN(speaking - between the first and second Verse of No. 7). Your humble servant! A real Russian, pushing everyone around! If everyone who's bored gets thrown out, I'm sure the guests would always be amused!

EISENSTEIN. (spricht) Wie Harmlos! Wenn einer nicht mehr trinken will, fliegt ihm die Flasche an den Kopf! Das sind allerdings nationale Eigentümlichkeiten, die man beachten muss!

ORLOFSKY. Schmeckt Ihnen der Madeira?

EISENSTEIN. Ausgezeichnet!

ORLOFSKY. Mir leider nicht! Früher wirkten noch derlei Reizmittel; jetzt aber mundet mir gar nichts mehr. Ich habe nicht einmal Appetit auf die Liebe.

EISENSTEIN. Oh, auf die Liebe habe ich noch immer gesegneten Appetit.

ORLOFSKY. (leert hastig sein Glas) Ach, ich möchte noch einmal jung werden!

EISENSTEIN. Wünschen Durchlaucht vielleicht noch einmal in den hochfürstlichen Windeln zu liegen?

ORLOFSKY. Ich möchte lachen, herzlich lachen, und das kann ich so selten. Aber Dr. Falke hat mir versprochen, dass ich heut über Sie lachen soll.

EISENSTEIN. (verblüfft) Über mich?

ORLOFSKY. Ja, über Sie! (zu Falke) Nicht wahr, Falke, wir werden über den Herrn Marquis lachen?

FALKE. Ich hoffe es, Durchlaucht!

EISENSTEIN. Wieso wollen Sie denn über mich.... (betrachtet sich von allen Seiten)

FALKE. (leise zu Orlofsky) Es ist alles besorgt.

EISENSTEIN. (für sich) Was flüstern sie da miteinander?

ADELE. (Orlofsky die leere Brieftasche überreichend) Mein Prinz, ich stelle Ihnen Ihr Portefeuille zurück; es ist leer!

IDA. Der gerissene Carikoni hat uns alles abgenommen.

EISENSTEIN. (Adele erblickend) Alle Wetter!

ORLOFSKY. Was gibt's?

EISENSTEIN. Das ist ja... (für sich) Das ist mein Stubenmädchen!

ADELE. (leise zu Ida) Mein gnädiger Herr!

IDA. Was sagst du?

EISENSTEIN. (für sich) Und noch dazu in der Robe meiner Frau!

ADELE. (zu Ida) Und die arme Frau glaubt, er schmachtet im Arrest!

FALKE. (stellt vor) Fräulein Olga...Fräulein Ida.... Herr Marquis Renard!

ADELE. (für sich) Jetzt heisst's alle Keckheit zusammennehmen!

IDA. Zeig, dass du Komödie spielen kannst!

EISENSTEIN. (zu Adele) Fräulein Olga heissen Sie?

ORLOFSKY. Marquis, Sie machen so ein verteufelt verdutztes Gesicht. Falke hat recht, ich werde lachen!

EISENSTEIN. (sucht sich zu fassen) Nur keine Blamage!

ORLOFSKY. Fräulein Olga scheint einen tiefen Eindruck auf Sie zu machen.

EISENSTEIN. O nein! Wieso? Ich glaubte nur...eine Ähnlichkeit...(entschlossen zu Adele) Mein Fräulein, sind Sie immer Fräulein Olga gewesen?

ADELE. Mein Herr Marquis, sind Sie immer Marquis Renard gewesen?

FALKE. Brava, ganz gut!

EISENSTEIN. Nein, diese Ähnlichkeit!

ADELE. Mit wem, mein Herr, mit wem?

EISENSTEIN. Mit...meinem Stubenmädchen!

ORLOFSKY, FALKE. (losplatzend) Hahaha!

ADELE. Ich einem Stubenmädchen ähnlich? Impertinent! Wollen Sie mich beleidigen?

EISENSTEIN. Beruhigen Sie sich! Das Stubenmädchen, dem Sie ähnlich sehen, ist ein reizendes, seltenes Exemplar, die Krone aller Stubenmädchen!

ADELE. Ach so, das ist etwas anderes!

ORLOFSKY. Immer besser! Hahaha!

EISENSTEIN. (speaking) How charming! If one stops drinking, a bottle flies at his head...Those are national peculiarities that should certainly be carefully observed!

ORLOFSKY. Do you enjoy the Madeira?

EISENSTEIN. Excellent!

ORLOFSKY. Unfortunately, I do not. Some time ago, such stimulants worked well, but I've no longer a taste for it. My appetite is gone, even for love.

EISENSTEIN. Oh, for love I have always a very healthy appetite!

ORLOFSKY. (emptying hastily his glass) Ah, to be young once more!

EISENSTEIN. Is your Highness longing to be once more in the royal diapers?

ORLOFSKY. I want to laugh, to laugh from the heart, and that I can so seldom do. But Dr. Falke promised me I shall laugh at you tonight.

EISENSTEIN. At me?

ORLOFSKY. Yes, at you! (to Falke) Is it not true, Falke, that we are going to laugh at the Marquis?

FALKE. I hope so, your Highness.

EISENSTEIN. How could you laugh at me? (looking at himself, from all angles)

FALKE. (softly to Orlofsky) Everything is arranged.

EISENSTEIN. (to himself) What are they whispering about?

ADELE. (handing Orlofsky the empty wallet) My Prince, I return your wallet. It's empty.

IDA. The clever Carikoni took it all from us.

EISENSTEIN. (seeing Adele) God in Heaven!

ORLOFSKY. What happened?

EISENSTEIN. But that...(to himself) That's my chambermaid!

ADELE. (softly to Ida) My master!

IDA. What are you saying?

EISENSTEIN. (to himself) And in my wife's evening dress!

ADELE. (to Ida) And his poor wife thinks he's languishing in jail!

FALKE. (introduces) Miss Olga.... Miss Ida ...... Marquis Renard!

ADELE. (to herself) Now I really need all my nerve.

IDA. Show them how well you can act!

EISENSTEIN. (to Adele) Your name is Miss Olga?

ORLOFSKY. Marquis, what a devilishly astonished face you make! Falke is right; I am going to laugh!

EISENSTEIN. (trying to control himself) I'll not be ridiculous!

ORLOFSKY. It seems Miss Olga has made quite an impression on you, Marquis?

EISENSTEIN. Oh, no! How so? I only thought...a resemblance...(decisively, to Adele) Miss, have you always been Miss Olga?

ADELE. My dear Marquis, have you always been Marquis Renard?

FALKE. Bravo, very good!

EISENSTEIN. No, the resemblance is so striking!

ADELE. To whom, Marquis, to whom?

EISENSTEIN. To.....to my chambermaid!

ORLOFSKY, FALKE. (bursting into laughter) Ha, ha, ha!

ADELE. I, resemble a chambermaid? How impertinent! Do you mean to insult me?

EISENSTEIN. Calm yourself! The chambermaid whom you resemble is a most unusual charming specimen, the princess of chambermaids!

ADELE. Ah, that's a little different!

ORLOFSKY. Better and better, Ha, ha, ha!

№ 8. ENSEMBLE und COUPLETS.

84

EISENSTEIN. (spricht) Alle Wetter, jetzt ist's aber genug mit dem Lachen! Ich bitte um Pardon, meine Herrschaften, seien Sie Grossmütig!

ADELE. Wenn Sie um Gnade bitten, sei Ihnen verziehen. Aber nehmen Sie sich in Zukunft vor schönen Kammerzofen in acht!

IVAN. (meldet) Der Chevalier Chargrin!

ORLOFSKY. (leise zu Falke) Chargrin?

FALKE. (ebenso) Der Gefängnisdirektor Frank.

ORLOFSKY. Ah so!

FALKE. (Frank entgegen). Ich heisse Sie willkommen im Namen Ihrer Durchlaucht!

ORLOFSKY. Willkommen, Chevalier!

FRANK. (in Balltoilette). Sie verzeihen, Durchlaucht, dass ich etwas spät....

ORLOFSKY. Ohne Umstände, meine Gäste sind bei mir zu Hause.

FALKE. (vorstellend). Chevalier Chargrin... Marquis Renard!

ORLOFSKY. Also Landsleute?

EISENSTEIN. (für sich). O verflucht, der redet vielleicht französisch mit mir!

FRANK. (schüttelt Eisenstein die Hand) J'ai l'honneur, Monsieur le Marquis!

EISENSTEIN. J'ai l'honneur... serviteur! (für sich) Will er noch mehr, gibt's ein Malhör!

FRANK. Vous êtes aussi Français?

EISENSTEIN. Aussi, aussi, aussi! (für sich) Aussi möcht ich!

FRANK. Je suis charmé de trouver un compatriot!

EISENSTEIN. (zu Falke) Ich bitte dich, mach, dass er mich mit dem Französischen in Ruhe lässt - ich bin damit am Ende.

FALKE. Wir bitten aber deutsch, meine Herrn!

IDA. Ach ja, uns ist die deutsche Konversation geläufiger!

EISENSTEIN. Ich spreche zwar mit einem Landsmann nicht gern deutsch, indes, da die Damen es wünschen, meinetwegen.

FRANK. (leise zu Falke). Ich danke Ihnen für den Titel "Chevalier"! Als Gefängnisdirektor kann ich doch in dieser Gesellschaft nicht auftreten!

EISENSTEIN. Sind Sie schon länger in diesem Badeort, Chevalier?

FRANK. Seit drei Tagen, Herr Marquis.

FALKE. Die Herren sind sich früher noch nicht begegnet?

EISENSTEIN. Nein, ich bedaure.

FRANK. Ich zeige mich selten öffentlich, ich bin ein grosser Freund von geschlossenen Zirkeln. In Zukunft aber hoffe ich....

EISENSTEIN. ....werden wir uns öfter sehen! (reicht ihm die Hand).

FRANK. (einschlagend). Und unsere Bekanntschaft fortsetzen!

FALKE. Ganz gewiss.

EISENSTEIN. (zu Falke). Ein liebenswürdiger Mann, dieser Chevalier!

FRANK. (ebenso zu Falke). Der Marquis gefällt mir ungemein!

FALKE. (zu Orlofsky). Was werden die Herren erst sagen, wenn sie sich näher kennenlernen!

ORLOFSKY. Sehr gut.

IDA. Warum soupieren wir denn aber nicht? Ich habe schon schrecklichen Hunger.

MEHRERE DAMEN. Ich auch! Ich auch!

MURRAY. Wir in Kanada haben niemals Hunger, nur Durst!

FALKE. Die Herrschaften müssen sich noch ein wenig gedulden. Wir erwarten noch eine Dame.

ALLE. Eine Dame?

EISENSTEIN. (speaking) By blazes, that's about enough laughing! I beg your pardon, ladies and gentlemen, please be generous!

ADELE. Since you beg my pardon, I shall forgive you. But in the future, be more cautious with beautiful chambermaids!

IVAN. (introducing). The Chevalier Chargrin!

ORLOFSKY. (softly to Falke) Chargrin?

FALKE. (same) The prison director, Frank!

ORLOFSKY. I see!

FALKE. (meeting Frank). Welcome, in the name of his Highness!

ORLOFSKY. Welcome, Chevalier.

FRANK. (in full evening dress) Forgive me for being so late, your highness.

ORLOFSKY. No formalities, my guests are here at home!

FALKE. (introducing). Chevalier Chargrin... Marquis Renard!

ORLOFSKY. Then you are compatriots?

EISENSTEIN. Damn, what if he speaks French to me?

FRANK. (shakes hands with Eisenstein) (with very poor accent) J'ai l'Honneur, Monsieur le Marquis.

EISENSTEIN. J'ai l'Honneur,... serviteur! (to himself) If he goes on, this will be tragic.

FRANK. Vous etes aussi Francais?

EISENSTEIN. Aussi, aussi, aussi. (to himself) Oh, see if I can get away!

FRANK. Je suis charme de trouver un compatriot.

EISENSTEIN. Please make him leave "this" Frenchman in peace - I've said everything I know!

FALKE. Please, gentlemen, let us speak English!

IDA. Oh, yes, we're used to more informal conversation.

EISENSTEIN. Though I am naturally reluctant to speak to a compatriot in English, I shall yield to the ladies' petition.

FRANK. (softly, to Falke) Thank you for the title "Chevalier". I couldn't very well appear in such a gathering as a warden!

EISENSTEIN. How long have you been at this resort, Chevalier?

FRANK. Ah, three days, Marquis.

FALKE. Have you gentlemen met before?

EISENSTEIN. No, I am sorry to say.

FRANK. I rarely show myself at parties. I prefer "closed circles". In future, though, I hope....

EISENSTEIN. I will see a great deal of you!

FRANK. And cement our friendship!

FALKE. Certainly!

EISENSTEIN. (to Falke) A charming chap, this Chevalier!

FRANK. (same). This Marquis impresses me very well!

FALKE. (to Orlofsky). What will the gentlemen say, when they learn to know each other better?

ORLOFSKY. Very good!

IDA. When can we eat? I'm starving!

SEVERAL LADIES. Me, too! Me, too!

MURRAY. In Canada, nobody starves. We just get thirsty all the time!

FALKE. Ladies and gentlemen, please be patient a moment more. We are still expecting a lady.

ALL. A lady?

FALKE. Ja, eine Dame, und zwar eine wirkliche Dame wegen der ich die Diskretion der ganzen Gesellschaft in Anspruch nehmen muss.

ALLE. Wieso?

CARIKONI. Das müssen Sie erklären!

FALKE. Es ist nämlich eine Dame aus den höchsten aristokratischen Kreisen, eine ungarische Gräfin, die gern unserem amüsanten Souper beiwohnen möchte, aber gewisse Rücksichten zu nehmen hat.

EISENSTEIN. Die Ärmste ist wohl verheiratet?

FALKE. Jawohl, und dazu an einem Mann, der so eifersüchtig ist, dass er seine Frau am liebsten im Zigarettenetui mittragen möchte. Obwohl nun ihr Krampus einige Tage entfernt von Madrid der süssen Ruhe pflegt, ist die Dame doch vorsichtig genug, so lustige Gesellschaft nur maskiert zu besuchen.

ALLE. Maskiert?

FALKE. Ja, und ich habe ihr versprochen, dass sie in vollem Vertrauen auf unsere Diskretion erscheinen könne. Schwören Sie mir also, ihre Maskenfreiheit zu achten.

ALLE. Wir schwören!

EISENSTEIN. Maskiert! Das ist interessant!

IDA. Wahrscheinlich ist sie hässlich!

MELANIE. Hat vielleicht nichts als ein Paar schöne Augen!

FAUSTINE. Und will uns damit Konkurrenz machen!

ALLE DAMEN. Lächerlich!

ORLOFSKY. (zu Falke). Hören Sie, die Lästerzungen sind schon in voller Tätigkeit!

FALKE. Ich schlage vor, dass die Herrschaften noch eine kleine Promenade im Garten machen.

ALLE. (durcheinander). Ja, ganz recht! Das wollen wir! Kommen Sie! (Die Gesellschaft verliert sich in den Garten).

ADELE. (zu Eisenstein, der sie noch immer fixiert). Mein Herr Marquis, wie lange soll ich Ihnen denn noch als Orientierungsplan dienen?

EISENSTEIN. (für sich). Diese Ähnlichkeit ist horrend! Sie ist aber dennoch viel hübscher als Adele. Ich muss experimentieren. (Manövriert mit seiner Uhr vor Adeles Augen).

FALKE. (zu Frank, auf Ida deutend). Herr Chevalier, hier ist eine Stelle vakant.

FRANK (Ida den Arm bietend). Habe ich keinen Refus zu befürchten, wenn ich mich um eine so schöne Anstellung bewerbe?

IDA. Es kommt darauf an, ob Sie solchem Amte gewachsen sind. (beide ab in den Garten)

EISENSTEIN. (lässt seine Uhr repetieren)

FALKE. Ah, du willst gewiss wieder wissen, wieviel's geschlagen hat?

ADELE. Welch niedliche, allerliebste Uhr!

EISENSTEIN. (ihr den Arm bietend und den andern folgend). Sie ist eigentlich eine Damenuhr. Vielleicht bin ich heute so glücklich, sie einer liebenswürdigen Künstlerin verehren zu dürfen!

FALKE. (allein). Der Spitzbube! Wenn ihm nur einmal das Experiment misslänge und der Köder an irgendeinem Gürtel hängenbliebe! - Ah, da ist schon die Frau, die hat sich beeilt! (Zieht sich etwas zurück).

FALKE. Yes, a lady, a real lady, and I must ask you all to promise me to be discreet.

ALL. Why?

CARIKONI. You must explain!

FALKE. It happens to be a lady of the highest aristocratic circles, a Hungarian countess, who would like to join our amusing supper, but we must allow her certain considerations.

EISENSTEIN. Poor woman, she must be married!

FALKE. Yes indeed, and to a man so jealous he'd like to carry her around in his cigarette case. Although the old dragon is away for a few days, in Madrid, the lady wishes to take the precaution, in visiting such a lively party, of wearing a mask.

ALL. A mask?

FALKE. Yes, and I gave her my word that she can count on our complete discretion. Therefore, I must ask you to swear to me that you will all respect her right to be masked.

ALL. We promise!

EISENSTEIN. Masked! How interesting!

IDA. She's probably very ugly!

MELANIE. She has probably nothing but her beautiful eyes!

FAUSTINE. And will use them to compete with us!

ALL LADIES. Ridiculous!

ORLOFSKY. (to Falke). Do you hear them? Already the gossip goes full swing!

FALKE. I propose that we all take a little promenade in the garden.

ALL. That's a good idea! That's what we'll do! Come on, let's go! (the group disappears into the garden)

ADELE. (to Eisenstein, who is still staring at her). My dear Marquis, how long must I serve you as an object of curiosity?

EISENSTEIN. (to himself). The resemblance is terrifying! She is really a lot prettier than Adele. I must try an experiment. (Dangles his watch before Adele's eyes).

FALKE. (to Frank, indicating Ida). Chevalier, here is a vacant place.

FRANK. (taking Ida's arm). I hope I shall not be refused if I apply for such an attractive position?

IDA. It all depends; are you eligible for high office? (both exit into the garden)

EISENSTEIN. (lets his watch chime)

FALKE. Ah, I see you're counting the happy hours again!

ADELE. Oh, what an adorable little watch!

EISENSTEIN. (offering her his arm, and following the others) It really is a ladies watch. Perhaps tonight I shall have the pleasure of presenting it to an adorable actress!

FALKE. (alone). The rascal! If only once his experiment would fail, and his bait stolen to hang from some little creature's belt! Ah, here comes his wife! I see she hurried! (draws back a little).

ROSALINDE. (in Balltoilette, eine schwarze Halbmaske in der Hand). So werde ich hoffentlich unerkannt bleiben, auch von meinem saubern Herrn Gemahl, der dieses Abendkleid noch nicht kennt!

FALKE. (tritt ihr entgegen). Ich bedaure, gnädige Frau.....

ROSALINDE. Ach, Sie, Herr Doktor! So wäre wirklich wahr, was Sie mir geschrieben haben?

FALKE. Ein Blick in den Garten wird Sie überzeugen. Sehen Sie dort Ihren Herrn Gemahl, wie er seinen Arrest abbüsst!

ROSALINDE. Am Arm einer Dame - abscheulich! Doch was ist das? Nein, ich irre mich nicht! Das ist ja Adele, mein Kammermädchen!

FALKE. Allerdings, das ist Adele, Ihr Kammermädchen!

ROSALINDE. In solche Gesellschaft geht er?!

FALKE. (scheinheilig). Mich hat er auch dazu verführt!

ROSALINDE. (maliziös). Armer Verführer! -Und wie sie sich in meiner Robe brüstet! Na warte, Mamsell, dir werde ich ein Rezept für deine alte Tante verschreiben!

FALKE. Nur heute nicht, gnädige Frau, ich bitte!

ROSALINDE. Besorgen Sie nichts! Das Pulverfass wird erst morgen explodieren, aber dann wird es einen fürchterlichen Krach geben!

FALKE. Pst, man kommt!

(Rosalinde setzt die Maske auf).

EISENSTEIN. (Arm in Arm mit Frank aus dem Garten). HAha, das ist eine köstliche Unterhaltung!

ROSALINDE. (für sich). Was seh ich? Auch der Gefängnisdirektor hier!

FRANK. Ihre Uhr, Marquis, ist ein wahrer Talisman!

ROSALINDE. (für sich). Für einen Marquis gibt sich der Spitzbube aus!

EISENSTEIN. Nicht wahr? Ja, ich habe ihr schon unzählige Eroberungen zu danken!

FALKE. Wenn das deine Frau wüsste!

EISENSTEIN. Haha, mein armes Weibchen träumt jetzt wahrscheinlich von ihrem Gabriel!

ROSALINDE. (für sich). Und ihr Gabriel macht sich lustig über sie!

FRANK. Sie wohnen in der Nähe, Marquis?

EISENSTEIN. Ganz in der Nähe; zehn Minuten von hier.... da rechts herum.

FRANK. Gerade wie ich...nur links herum. Sonderbar, dass wir uns bis jetzt noch nirgends getroffen haben! Aber in Zukunft hoffe ich, Sie recht bald bei mir zu sehen.

FALKE. (lacht). Jawohl, und das schon morgen!

EISENSTEIN. (bietet Frank die Hand). Wir wollen Freunde sein!

FRANK. Von Herzen gern!

EISENSTEIN, FRANK. (umarmen sich). Ein Herz und eine Seele!

FALKE. (lacht laut). Haha!

EISENSTEIN. Was gibt's denn wieder zu lachen?

FALKE. (indem er auf Rosalinde deutet). Ich finde es immer lächerlich, wenn Männer sich in Gegenwart schöner Frauen umarmen.

FRANK. Alle Wetter....

EISENSTEIN. Das ist wohl....?

FALKE. Die ungarische Gräfin, von der ich sprach. Sie soll bezaubernd schön sein.

EISENSTEIN. Donnerwetter, das wäre was für mich! Überlasst sie mir, meine Herren!

ROSALINDA. (in evening gown, a black mask in her hand). I hope I won't be recognized, especially by my swine of a husband. I'm glad I didn't tell him about this new dress.

FALKE. (advancing to receive her). I am so sorry, dear lady.....

ROSALINDA. Ah, it's you, Doctor! So it is really true, what you wrote me?

FALKE. A glance into the garden should convince you. There you will see how your husband is paying his debt to society!

ROSALINDA. A girl on his arm! How dreadful! But who is that girl? No, I am not mistaken! That is Adele, my own chambermaid!

FALKE. It is Adele, your own chambermaid!

ROSALINDA. Is that the sort of company he's keeping?

FALKE. (hypocritically). He's even seduced me to it!

ROSALINDA. (maliciously). The Great Seducer! And how she is showing off, in my dress! Just you wait, little lady, I'll prescribe you a cure for your old aunt!

FALKE. Only not this evening, dear lady, I beg you!

ROSALINDA. Don't worry! I won't start shooting until morning - but then there'll be quite an explosion!

FALKE. Psst, some one's coming!

(Rosalinda puts on the mask).

EISENSTEIN. (arm in arm with Frank, coming from the garden). Ha, ha, this is wonderfully entertaining!

ROSALINDA. (to herself). Can I believe my eyes? The prison director here, too?

FRANK. Your watch is a real gem, Marquis!

ROSALINDA. (to herself). The rogue is pretending to be a Marquis!

EISENSTEIN. Isn't it, though? Yes, I owe many a conquest to it.

FALKE. If your wife only knew!

EISENSTEIN. Ha, ha, ha, my poor little wife, probably dreaming sweetly right now of her Gabriel!

ROSALINDA. (to herself). And her Gabriel is making fun of her!

FRANK. Do you live in the neighborhood, Marquis?

EISENSTEIN. Oh, very near; not ten minutes away, just there on the right...

FRANK. So do I...only on the left. Isn't it amazing we haven't met before? But in future, I hope you will visit me, very soon.

FALKE. (laughing). He will indeed--tomorrow morning!

EISENSTEIN. (offers his hand to Frank). We shall be friends!

FRANK. With all my heart!

EISENSTEIN, FRANK. (embracing each other). We shall never part!

FALKE. (laughs aloud). Ha, ha!

EISENSTEIN. Now what is so funny?

FALKE. (indicating Rosalinda). I always find it funny to see two men embrace when there is a lovely lady present!

FRANK. Good Heaven!

EISENSTEIN. Then that is.....?

FALKE. The Hungarian countess, of whom I was speaking. She is said to be ravishingly beautiful.

EISENSTEIN. By heaven, that should be something for me! Leave her to me, gentlemen!

FALKE. Meinetwegen, du Nimmersatt!
FRANK. Ich habe auch nichts dagegen. (nimmt Falke unterm Arm).
EISENSTEIN. In zehn Minuten ist sie mein! Mir widersteht keine!
FALKE. Viel Glück, Marquis, viel Glück!
FRANK. (im Abgehen zu Falke). Dieser Marquis ist ein ebenso lustiger Freund wie Ihr Eisenstein, lieber Doktor!

EISENSTEIN. (der das letzte gehört hat, für sich). Ich bin gerade so lustig wie ich? Was weiss er denn von Eisenstein? Er kennt mich ja als Eisenstein gar nicht!
ROSALINDE. (tritt auf Eisenstein zu, ergreift ihn beim Arm, sieht ihm lange und scharf ins Gesicht).
EISENSTEIN. (verlegen). Nanu?
ROSALINDE. (lässt von ihm ab, grimmig für sich). Wie gern ich ihn beim Schopfe nehmen möchte; aber ich darf mich nicht verraten!
EISENSTEIN. (für sich). Sapperlot, die scheint Feuer zu haben! Ungarisch Blut! An das Märchen von der hohen Gräfin und der hohen Aristokratie glaube ich nicht. Sie wird auf die Uhr anbeissen wie die andern! (Zieht die Uhr hervor).
ROSALINDE. (für sich). Was hat er vor? Ah, er sprach ja vorhin von seiner Uhr, der er unzählige Eroberungen verdankt!
EISENSTEIN. (lässt die Uhr repetieren).
ROSALINDE. (mit verstellter Stimme). Welch allerliebste Damenuhr!
EISENSTEIN. Ja, sie ist niedlich.
ROSALINDE. Wo kauft man denn so niedliche Uhren?
EISENSTEIN. Ich habe sie beim Juwelier gekauft, um sie einer Liebenswürdigen Künstlerin als Zeichen meiner Huldigung darzubringen.
ROSALINDE. In der nächsten Woche werde ich debütieren.
EISENSTEIN. (für sich). Also nicht Gräfin, sondern Künstlerin!
ROSALINDE. Der Herr Intendant hat mir viel Schönes auf der Probe gesagt.
EISENSTEIN. (für sich). Auf mein Experiment kann ich mich verlassen!
ROSALINDE. Um Vergebung, Herr Marquis, sind Sie verheiratet?
EISENSTEIN. Ich? Wie können Sie so etwas glauben!
ROSALINDE. (für sich). Du Erzheuchler!
EISENSTEIN. Erlauben Sie auch mir eine Frage: wäre es nicht endlich an der Zeit, ein wenig die Maske zu lüften?
ROSALINDE. Heute nicht; aber morgen will ich mich Ihnen ohne Maske zeigen.
EISENSTEIN. (ärgerlich). Morgen ist es nicht möglich.
ROSALINDE. Warum nicht morgen?
EISENSTEIN. Ich... ich... habe Sitzung morgen.
ROSALINDE. Sitzung?
EISENSTEIN. Eine geheime Sitzung unter Ausschluss der Öffentlichkeit!
ROSALINDE. Vielleicht werde ich auch dabeisein!
EISENSTEIN. Sie scherzen! (für sich). Sie ist wirklich zum Entzücken! (lässt die Uhr repetieren).
ROSALINDE. (für sich). Wenn ich nur die Uhr erwischen könnte! Das wäre ein treffliches Corpus delicti!

FALKE. It's all right with me, you insatiable devil!
FRANK. I'll make no objection! (takes Falke by the arm).
EISENSTEIN. In ten minutes, she'll be mine! Who can resist me?
FALKE. Good luck, Marquis, lots of luck!
FRANK. (while exiting with Falke). This Marquis seems to be just as jolly as your friend Eisenstein, my good doctor!

EISENSTEIN. (who has heard the last remark, to himself). I am as jolly as myself? What does he know about Eisenstein? He didn't know me when I was Eisenstein, either!
ROSALINDA. (approaching Eisenstein, takes his arm and looks long and intensely into his face).
EISENSTEIN. (embarassed). Well?
ROSALINDA. (lets him go, disgustedly to herself) How I'd love to tear his hair out! But I dare not give myself away.
EISENSTEIN. (to himself). By Jove, she seems to be full of fire! Hungarian blood! But I don't believe that fairy-tale about the "countess" and the high aristocracy! She'll fall for the watch, just like all the rest of them! (takes out the watch).
ROSALINDA. (to herself). What's he trying now? Ah, he was talking before about his watch, to which he owes his countless conquests!
EISENSTEIN. (lets the watch chime).
ROSALINDA. (with disguised voice) What an adorable ladies watch!
EISENSTEIN. Yes, isn't it charming?
ROSALINDA. Where could one purchase such a charming little watch?
EISENSTEIN. Oh, I picked it up at a special jeweller's, so I could present a little token of my admiration to some especially lovable actress!
ROSALINDA. I shall make my debut next week!
EISENSTEIN. (to himself). So, she's no countess, but an actress!
ROSALINDA. The theatre director gave me many compliments on my audition!
EISENSTEIN. (to himself). Now I am sure of my experiment's success!
ROSALINDA. Excuse me, Marquis, but are you married?

EISENSTEIN. I? How could you think such a thing?
ROSALINDA. (to herself). The arch-hypocrite!
EISENSTEIN. Allow me also a question: has the time come for you to lift your mask, just a little?

ROSALINDA. Not tonight; but tomorrow the masks will all be off!
EISENSTEIN. (annoyed). Tomorrow it will be impossible.
ROSALINDA. Why not tomorrow?
EISENSTEIN. I... I... I have an appointment tomorrow.
ROSALINDA. An appointment?
EISENSTEIN. Yes, a private appointment, behind closed doors.
ROSALINDA. Perhaps I shall come with you!
EISENSTEIN. You are joking! (to himself). She is really enchanting! (lets his watch chime)
ROSALINDA. (to herself). If I could only capture that watch! What a perfect corpus delicti!

№ 9. DUETT.

94

dan-ke von Her-zen! Be - lie-ben zu scher-zen!
thank you with plea-sure! You're jok - ing! This trea-sure!

Ich woll-te nur!
Do give it back!

Ach!
Ah!

Sie ist nicht in's Netz ge - gan - gen,
She has won the game I start - ed,

hat die Uhr mir ab - ge-fan - gen; die - ser Spass ist et - was theu-er,
now my watch and I are part - ed; what a dread-ful price I'm pay-ing,

MELANIE (zu Falke). Den Spass müssen Sie uns erzählen, Doktor!

FAUSTINE (bemerkt Rosalinde). Ah, da ist ja das Mädchen aus der Fremde!

IDA. Die interessante Unbekannte, die uns der Doktor angekündigt!

ADELE. Ich wäre doch sehr begierig, ihr ins Auge zu blicken.

DIE DAMEN. Ich auch! Ich auch!

ADELE. Wir wollen den Sturm wagen. (zu Rosalinde). Schöne Unbekannte, wenn Sie nicht gar zu hässlich...

FAUSTINE. ...oder die Prinzessin mit dem Totenkopf sind....

ADELE...möchten wir Sie bitten, sich zu demaskieren!

ALLE. Demaskieren! Demaskieren!

ORLOFSKY. Halt, meine Herrschaften, das ist wider die Abrede. In meiner Villa hat jede Dame das Recht, sich zu verhüllen oder zu enthüllen, so weit es ihr beliebt. (zu Rosalinde) Ganz ungeniert, meine Holde!

EISENSTEIN (nach seiner Uhr blickend) Oh, die Holde geniert sich gar nicht. Meine Uhr ist futsch!

ADELE. Übrigens könnte ich zehn gegen eins wetten, dass sie keine Ungarin ist. Eine Dame jenseits der Leitha hat mehr Feuer und wäre in unserer Gesellschaft längst explodiert!

ORLOFSKY. Und dennoch ist sie eine Ungarin!

MELANIE. Und wer verbürgt uns das, Durchlaucht?

ROSALINDE. Die Musik verbürgt es!

ALLE. Die Musik?

ROSALINDE. Ja, die nationalen Töne meines Vaterlands mögen für mich sprechen!

MELANIE (to Falke). You must explain the joke, Doctor!

FAUSTINE (noticing Rosalinda). Ah, here is the exotic foreigner!

IDA. The fascinating mystery-lady, whom the Doctor announced!

ADELE. I'd like to look her in the eyes!

THE LADIES. Me, too! Me, too!

ADELE. Let's try the attack! (to Rosalinda). Lovely Mystery-Lady, if you are not too hideous....

FAUSTINE. ...or the faceless wonder..

ADELE.... Allow us to ask you to lift your mask!

ALL. Unmask! Unmask!

ORLOFSKY. Stop, dear ladies! You are breaking the agreement. In my villa, every lady has the right to cover... or uncover.... as much as she likes. (to Rosalinda) Without embarassment, my fair one.

EISENSTEIN. (looking toward his watch). She's not embarassed, and she's not fair. She kept my watch.

ADELE. I'll give you ten to one she's not even Hungarian. A lady from behind the paprika curtain has more fire; she'd have exploded long ago in this company!

ORLOFSKY. She does not look hungry, either, and still she is Hungarian.

MELANIE. Who can guarantee that, your Highness?

ROSALINDA. Let music be my guarantee!

ALL. Music?

ROSALINDA. Certainly, let the melodies of my fatherland speak for me!

Nº 10. CSÁRDÁS.

Frischka.

Feu- er, Le-ben lust, schwellt äch-te Un-gar-brust, hei! zum
Fier- y, full of zest, swells ev'- ry Mag-yar breast, hei! Come

Tan-ze schnell! Csar-das tönt so hell! Brau- nes Mäg-de-lein, musst mei-ne
dance to-night! Csar-das sounds so bright! Dark- eyed gyp-sy girl, join in the

Tanz'-rin sein; reich' den Arm ge-schwind, dun-kel- äu-gig kind!
joy- ous whirl, danc- -ing, light and wild, love-ly laugh-ing child! -

Zum Fie- del- klin- gen, ho ha, tönt jauch- zend
fid- dles are strum- ming, ho ha, ju- bi- lant

Sin- -gen: ho ha, Mit dem Sporn ge-klirrt, wenn dann die
hum- -ming: ho ha, When he clanks his spurs, eyes shin-ing

Maid ver-wirrt senkt zur Erd' den Blick, das ver-kün-det Glück! Durst'ge
in - to hers, in her blush-ing glance, he can read ro - mance! Thirsts are

Ze - cher, greift zum Be - cher, lasst ihn kreisen, lasst ihn
grow - ing, wine is flow - ing, pass the bot-tle 'round the

krei-sen schnell von Hand zu Hand! Schlürft das Feu - er im To-
cir - cle quick from hand to hand! Gai - ly drink-ing, nev - er-

-kay - er! bringt ein Hoch aus dem Va - ter-land! Ha!!
think-ing, with a hail for our fa - ther-land! Ha!!

rit.

rit.

ALLE. (applaudierend). Brava! Bravissima!
MELANIE. (zu Falke). Was ist's mit dem versproch-
nen Spass, Doktor?
FALKE. Sie meinen?
RAMUSIN. Die Geschichte von der Fledermaus!
EISENSTEIN. Von der Fledermaus ist die Rede? Das
war ja meine Komödie, in der ich dem armen
Doktor die Titelrolle zuteile. Ein köstlicher
Spass, dem er zum Opfer fiel. Seine Blamage
kann er euch doch nicht selbst beschreiben!
FAUSTINE. So erzählen Sie, Marquis!
EISENSTEIN. (zu Falke) Darf ich?
FALKE. Ohne Bedenken!
EISENSTEIN. Vor drei Jahren waren Falke und ich
noch ein paar lustige, fidele Brüder...
ADELE. Oh, das seid ihr noch!
ROSALINDE. (leise zu Falke) Unverschämt!
FALKE. Pst! Verraten Sie sich nicht!
EISENSTEIN. Wir wohnten beide in dem Städtchen
Weinberg. Falke war damals schon Notar, ich
aber war noch unverheiratet.
ALI BEY. Wie? Sie sind verheiratet, Marquis?
ROSALINDE. Entsetzlich! Eine Frau haben Sie? Oh,
meine Hoffnungen!
EISENSTEIN. Hoffen Sie deswegen ungeniert, holde
Uhrabzwickerin! Meine Frau ist steinalt und
hässlich wie eine Nachteule.
ROSALINDE. (zu Falke). Was für ein schmeichel-
haftes Porträt!
EISENSTEIN. Auf einem Schlosse, zwei Meilen von
unserem Städtchen, gab die Herrschaft einen
Maskenball, zu dem wir auch eingeladen waren.
Ich maskierte mich als Papillon, und der Dok-
tor als Fledermaus.
ALLE. Falke als Fledermaus! Haha!
EISENSTEIN. Ganz eingenäht in ein braunes Fell, lange Krallen, breite Flügel und einen ungeheuren
gelben Schnabel...
MURRAY. Bei uns in Kanada haben die Fledermäuse
keine gelben Schnäbel!
EISENSTEIN. Das ist möglich, aber er hatte einen und
sah famos aus als Gelbschnabel.
ALLE. Wir glauben's.
EISENSTEIN. Wir fuhren in einem Fiaker miteinander
auf den Ball, unterhielten uns köstlich; ich wollte mir jedoch einen Extrajux leisten und trank
unserem Doktor fleissig zu, so dass er gegen Morgen kanonenvoll betrunken war. Dann legte ich
ihn in den Wagen, fuhr mit ihm in ein kleines
Gehölz, bettete ihn unter einen Baum und mach-
te mich aus dem Staub. Er merkte davon nichts,
sondern schlief wie ein Murmeltier.
ALLE. Haha, der arme Doktor!
EISENSTEIN. Als er endlich erwachte, musste er bei
hellem, lichtem Tag als Fledermaus zum Gau-
dium aller Schulkinder in die Stadt marschieren,
bis er endlich unter starker Begleitung seine Woh-
nung erreichte.
ALLE. Hahaha!
EISENSTEIN. Seitdem wurde er in Weinberg nur noch
Dr. Fledermaus genannt.
IDA. Und er hat sich nicht gerächt für den groben
Spass?
EISENSTEIN. Oh, ich bin auf meiner Hut!
FALKE. Aufgeschoben ist nicht aufgehoben!
Vielleicht erleben wir schon morgen, wer von
uns den ersten Preis als Spassmacher verdient.

ALL. (applauding). Bravo! Bravissimo!
MELANIE. (to Falke). What about the joke you pro-
mised, Doctor?
FALKE. What do you mean?
RAMUSIN. The story of the bat?
EISENSTEIN. Are you talking about the Bat? That was
my little comedy, in which I gave the title role
to the poor Doctor. It was a great joke, of which
he was the victim. He never could describe to
you how ridiculous he was!
FAUSTINE. Then why don't you tell us?
EISENSTEIN. (to Falke) May I?
FALKE. Be my guest!
EISENSTEIN. Three years ago, Dr. Falke and I were
a pair of loyal, jolly brothers.
ADELE. Oh, that you still are!
ROSALINDA. (softly to Falke). Completely shameless!
FALKE. Psst! Don't give yourself away!
EISENSTEIN. We were living in Weinberg. Falke was
already a notary, but I was not yet married.
ALI BEY. What? Are you married now, Marquis?
ROSALINDA. Isn't that appalling? You have a wife?
Oh, my illusions! My hopes!
EISENSTEIN. Hope away, my lovely time-keeper!
My wife is petrified from age and ugly as sin!
ROSALINDA. (softly to Falke). Always the flatterer!
EISENSTEIN. We were invited to a castle, two miles
from town, for a masked ball. I went disguised
as a butterfly, and the Doctor was a bat.
ALL. Falke as a bat! Ha, ha, ha!
EISENSTEIN. All sewed up into a brown skin, with long
claws and enormous wings, and a monstrous yel-
low beak....
MURRAY. In Canada, bats don't have a yellow beak.
EISENSTEIN. That may well be, but he had one, and it
became him very well, too!
ALL. We believe it! We can imagine!
EISENSTEIN. We went to the ball in the same coach,
and we had a splendid time. But I wanted a little extra amusement, so I gave the good doctor a
few too many, so that by dawn, he was out like a
stone. Then I got him into the coach, and took
him off to a little park, arranged him carefully
under a tree, and took my leave. He never moved
a muscle; he was sleeping like a dormouse!
ALL. Ha, ha, ha! the poor Doctor!
EISENSTEIN. The school children finally woke him up
with their laughing, and they followed him all the
way home, in clear broad daylight, making a tre-
mendous parade and shouting with laughter!
ALL. Ha, ha, ha!
EISENSTEIN. Ever since that, everyone in Weinberg
calls him the batty doctor!
IDA. Did he never get revenge for such a painful trick?
EISENSTEIN. Oh, I am always on my guard!
FALKE. Postponed does not mean cancelled! Who knows,
by tomorrow another joker may wear the crown!

FRANK. Marquis, diese Fledermaus Idee war süperb!
  Einen solchen Spass kann nur ein Marquis erfinden!
FALKE. (zur Gesellschaft). Trinkt dem Marquis und
  dem Chevalier fleissig zu, ich bitte euch.
ORLOFSKY. Vorwärts, zu Tische, meine Damen und
  Herren!
ALLE. Zu Tisch, zu Tische!
  (Man setzt sich zur Tafel. Diener servieren).
EISENSTEIN. Wird auch jetzt noch
  nicht die Maske fallen?
ROSALINDE. Auch jetzt noch nicht, aber morgen!
1. Diener (zu Eisenstein). Château Laroie oder Champagner?
EISENSTEIN. Beides, mein Freund, beides!
2. Diener (zu Frank). Château Laroie oder Champagner?
FRANK. Nicht "oder", sondern "und"! Gleiches
  Recht für beide!
EISENSTEIN. (singt). "Freut euch des Lebens...."
MELANIE. Erlaubt Ihnen denn aber auch Ihre Marquise, sich hier Ihres Lebens zu freuen?
EISENSTEIN. Oh, Sie liebe Unschuld! Glauben Sie
  denn, ich sage ihr immer, wohin ich gehe?
  Meine Alte glaubt mich jetzt ganz wo anders.
ROSALINDE. (erbost) Seine Alte!
MELANIE. Sie soll leben, Ihre Alte!
ALLE. (heben die Gläser) Hoch!
ORLOFSKY. (auf Rosalinde deutend). Auch die schöne Helena dort!
ALLE. Hoch, hoch!
EISENSTEIN. Vielleicht hat sie auch einen recht
  dummen Menelaus!
ORLOFSKY. Sagt mir doch, Kinder, woran liegt es,
  dass die Soupers auf dem Theater das Publikum
  so wenig amüsieren?
ADELE. Weil das Publikum mit trockenem Munde zusehen muss!
FALKE. Um auf dem Theater ein amüsantes Souper
  darzustellen, müsste man auch dem Publikum
  Champagner servieren lassen und jedem Herrn
  erlauben, seine Nachbarin zu umarmen!

DIE HERREN. Wie wir zum Beispiel! (Umarmen ihre
  Damen).
ORLOFSKY. (erhebt sich, das Glas in der Hand). Champagner, König aller Weine! Hoch die sprudelnde
  Majestät und ihre Untertanen!
ALLE. Hoch!

FRANK. Marquis, your batty idea was superb! Only a
  Marquis could have thought of it!
FALKE. (to the others). A toast to the Marquis and also to
  the Chevalier, if you please!
ORLOFSKY. And now, ladies and gentlemen, let us dine!

ALL. Let's dine, let's dine!
  (all sit down to table. Servants begin serving).
EISENSTEIN. (to Rosalinda). Won't you take that mask off
  now?
ROSALINDA. Not now, but tomorrow!
1st servant (to Eisenstein) Chateau Laroie or Champagne?

EISENSTEIN. Both, my friend, both!
2nd servant (to Frank). Chateau Laroie or Champagne?

FRANK. Not "or", but "and"! Equal rights for all!

EISENSTEIN. (sings). "Live a life of pleasure".....
MELANIE. But does your Marquise let you live this life
  of pleasure here?
EISENSTEIN. Ah, my darling Innocent! Do you think I
  always tell her where I'm going? The old woman
  thinks I'm in quite a different place!
ROSALINDA. (indignant). The old woman?
MELANIE. Long life to your old lady!
ALL. (raise their glasses). Hail!
ORLOFSKY. (indicating Rosalinda). Also to the beautiful
  Helen beside you!
ALL. Hail, hail!
EISENSTEIN. Perhaps she, too, has a stupid Menelaus!

ORLOFSKY. Tell me, chidren, why is it that a party onstage amuses the actors more than the audience?

ADELE. Because watching the actors drink makes them
  thirsty!
FALKE. To make a stage supper amusing, one must serve
  champagne to the audience- and allow the gentlemen to embrace their neighbors!

GENTLEMEN. And follow our example! (embracing
  their ladies).
ORLOFSKY. (rises, glass in hand). To Champagne, the
  King of all wines! Long live his sparkling Majesty, and all his subjects!
ALL. Hail!

№ 11. FINALE II.

112

114

FALKE.

ich's auch müssen! Folgt mei - nem Bei-spiel; das Glas zur Hand, und Je - der sing' zum
not be miss-ing! Now fol - low me, raise your glass on high, and toast the one who's

Nachbar ge-wandt: _____
stand-ing near-by:

Allegretto moderato.

Brü-der-lein, Brü-der-lein und Schwester-lein
Bro-ther-hood, bro-ther-hood and sis - ter-hood, ——

— wol-len Al-le wir sein, stimmt mit mir ein! Brü-der-lein, Brü-der-lein und
to each oth-er we sing, as lov - ers should, bro-ther-hood, bro-ther-hood and

Schwester -lein lasst das trau - te "Du" uns schen - ken für die
sis - ter-hood, with our love we con - quer sor - row. For e-

122

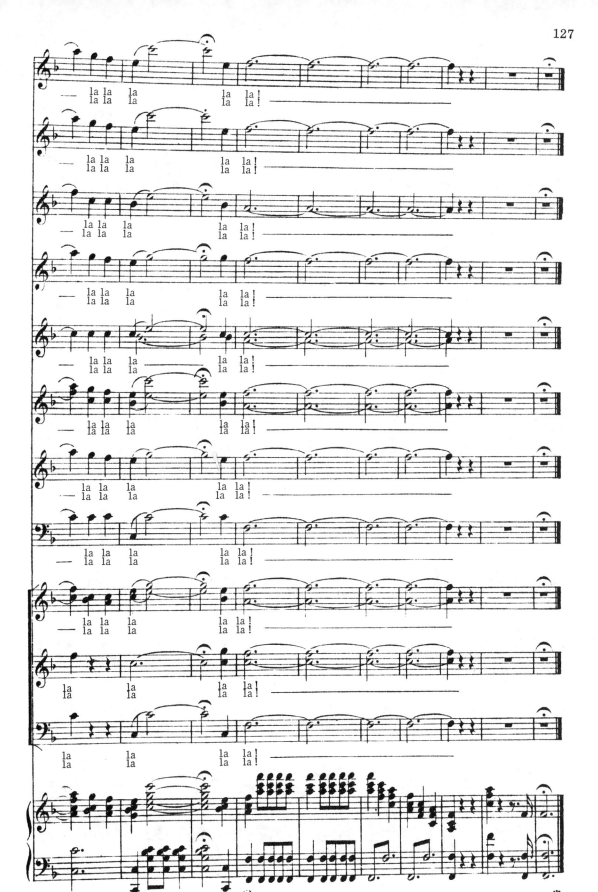

BALLET.

Allegretto moderato.

PIANO.

Allegro.

Allegretto.
(Schottisch.) (Scottish)

130

Allegretto molto moderato.

(Russian)
(Russisch.

Tempo di Polka.

SOPRAN.
ALT.

TENOR.
BASS.

Mar- ian-ka, komm und tanz me hier! Heut
Mar- ian-ka, come and dance viz me, al -

(Bohemian)
(Böhmisch.)

Tempo di Polka.

132

To - je hes-ki mu-sitschku, auf Trum-pet-tel, Cla-ri-net-tel, so wie ces-ky
To - je hes-ki mu-sitschku, with trum-pet-tel, Cla-ri-net-tel, so the czech mu-

Mu - si - kant blast me in kein an-dre Land. Mar -
si - cians, play, no one else can play that way. Mar -

ian-ka, komm und tanz' me' hier! Heut ist's schon schetzko jed-no, mir! Me' tanzens Pol-ka
ian-ka, come and dance wiz me! Al-read-y schetzko jed-no, see? Ve dance a pol-ka

al - le Zwei, wo is - se Hetz is Böhm' da-bei! Mar-ian-ka, komm und tanz' me' hier! Heut
me and you, vhat is a fun, Bo-hem-ians do! Mar-ian-ka, come and dance wiz me! Al-

134

ist's schon schetz- ko jed-no mir; me tan - zens Pol-ka al - le Zwei; wo
-read - y schetz-ko jed-no, see? ve dance a pol-ka me and you; vhat

is - se Hetz, is Bohm da-bei!
is a fun, bo - hem-ians do!

Allegro maestoso.   (Hungarian)
                                     (Ungarisch.)

Più Allegro.

138

139

Alle SOLI und CHOR.

Lie - be und Wein giebt uns Se - lig - keit; ging's durch das Le - ben so flott, wie
Float-ing on mus-ic and love and wine, life ev - er-last-ing would be such

Lie - be und Wein giebt uns Se - lig - keit; ging's durch das Le - ben so flott, wie
Float-ing on mus-ic and love and wine, life ev - er-last-ing would be such

Lie - be und Wein giebt uns Se - lig - keit; ging's durch das Le - ben so flott, wie
Float-ing on mus-ic and love and wine, life ev - er-last-ing would be such

heut, wär' je-de Stun - de der Lust ge - weiht !(Eisenst. und Frank treffen walzend)
bliss, if all our nights could be passed like this! (Eisenst. and Frank meet waltzing)

heut, wär' je-de Stun - de der Lust ge - weiht!
bliss, if all our nights could be passed like this!

heut, wär' je-de Stun - de der Lust ge - weiht!
bliss, if all our nights could be passed like this!

EISENST. (sich an Frank haltend.) (leaning on Frank)   FRANK.

Du bist meine Stütze, Freund! Ja, Dei - ne Stütze für's Le-ben!
Dear friend, I depend on you! Trust me, I never will fail you!

ROSAL.

Welch' ein rüh - rend Wie - der-sehn wird das im Ar -
What a great sur - prise for you when your new-found

ORLOF.

Welch' ein rüh - rend Wie - der-sehn wird das im Ar -
What a great sur - prise for you when your new-found

FALKE.

Welch' ein rüh - rend Wie - der-sehn wird das im Ar -
What a great sur - prise for you when your new-found

140

Alle SOLI und CHOR.

FRANK (zu Eisenstein)
(to Eisenstein)

Brü-derl, brü-derl, meine Uhr geht schlecht; schau, wie viel's auf Dei-ner ist.
Broth-er, broth-er, is my watch too slow? Tell me, what does your clock say?

EISENST.(nach seiner Uhr suchend)
(fumbling for his watch)

Brü - derl, meine geht auch nicht recht, weil sie schon ge -
Bro - ther, mine runs too fast, you know, for to - night it

(zu ROSAL.)
(to ROSAL.)

gan - gen ist. Hol - de, hier vor Al - len lass die
ran a - way. Love - ly one, I ask you, will you

Mas - ke end - lich fal - len, dass ich seh, wen ich be -
let us now un - mask you? let me see who shared my

ROSAL.(seine Hand ergreifend)
(taking his hand)

siegt und wer mei - ne Uhr ge - kriegt.
fun when my heart and watch were won.

142

144

146

(Diener bringen verschiedene Röcke und Hüte, die nicht passen)
(servants bring various capes and hats, none od which fit)

148

la la la la la la la la la!

weiht, dann blei-bet je-de Stund' der Lust ge - weiht!
bliss, if on-ly all our nights were passed like this!

weiht, dann blei-bet je-de Stund' der Lust ge - weiht!
bliss, if on-ly all our nights were passed like this!

weiht, dann blei-bet je-de Stund' der Lust ge - weiht!
bliss, if on-ly all our nights were passed like this!

(Eisenstein und Frank, die sich während des letzten Tempo Arm in Arm schwankend in den Hintergrund
(Eisenstein and Frank, during the last tempo, have staggered to the background ....

bewegten, werden dort von Tanzenden umringt.) während der Vorhang fällt.
where they are surrounded by dancers) as the curtain falls ....

Ende des zweiten Aktes
End of Act II

THIRD ACT
Dritter Akt.

Kanzlei des Gefängnisdirektors Frank. Im Hintergrund blickt man ins Vorzimmer. Links ein Fenster.
Auf beiden Seiten Türen. Rechts ein Schreibtisch
mit Teegeschirr, Wasserflasche, usw.

Office of the prison director, Frank. In the background, an ante-chamber is visible. At left is a
window; doors on both sides. Right is a desk with a
carafe of water and a tea-set.

No. 12. ENTREACT

No. 12 ENTR'ACTE

FROSCH (schliesst mit einem grossen Schlüsselbund die Mitteltüre auf, tritt mit einer brennenden Laterne in der Hand ziemlich betrunken ein).

ALFRED (singt hinter der Szene). Täubchen, holdes Täubchen mein (usw.)

FROSCH. Hoho, das ist ein fideles Gefängnis. Der Gefangene auf Numero 12 singt schon wieder. Ich bin erst seit ein paar Tagen mit dem Herrn Direktor hierher versetzt worden, aber es gefällt mir ganz gut. So ein fideles Gefängnis wie hier ist mir noch gar nicht vorgekommen. Und der Slibowitz, der ist hier auch sehr gut! Ja, ich habe gefunden, dass er hier sogar noch besser ist! Im Kopf hab ich nichts, der ganze Geist hat sich in die Stiefel gesenkt, darum sind sie so schwer. Und dann ist mir, als hör ich immer Musik!

ALFRED (hinter der Szene trällert wieder).

FROSCH. So lustig und fidel kommt mir hier alles vor. Ist das der Slibowitz? (horcht.) Nein, das ist der Gefangene von Numero 12, der singt schon wieder. (ruft.) Ruhe, Ruhe, mein Herr! Das Singen ist gegen die Hausordnung! Na wart, verdammter Slibowitz! (stolpert ab.) Verflucht fidel ist's hier im Gefängnis!

FROGG (opens the middle door with an enormous keyring, and appears with a lit lantern in his hand; he is quite intoxicated.)

ALFRED (sings backstage). Darling Dove that flew away, etc....

FROGG. Hoho, this is a jolly jail. The prisoner in number 12 is singing again. I've only been here a few days, since I was transferred with the Director, but it certainly seems to agree with me. I never saw such a jolly jail. And the liquor here agrees with me, too! Yes, I like it better and better! My head's as clear as can be... my brain has relaxed itself right down to my boots. That must be why they're so heavy! And then I keep hearing strange music!

ALFRED (backstage, sings anew).

FROGG. How pleasant and jolly everything seems to be! Could it be the alcohol? (listening) No, it's the prisoner in number 12 singing again. (calls) Quiet, quiet, sir! Singing is against the rules! Wait right there, you bloody bottle! (staggers off) It certainly is damned jolly, here in jail!

№ 13. MELODRAM.
No. 13 MELODRAMA

Moderato.

(Frank erscheint, - den Paletot
(Frank appears, - his overcoat

PIANO.   pp

schief zu geknöpft, den Hut tief in die Augen gedrückt, schwanken Schrittes. Er sucht vergeblich sei-
buttoned awry, his hat pushed down over his eyes; his steps stagger.   He tries in vain

nem Gange Festigkeit zu geben. Nach vorn gekommen nimmt er den Hut ab und schleudert ihn in die
to walk straight. Having reached the front, he takes off his hat and throws it in the corner)

Walzer-Tempo.

Zimmerecke)
acceler.   ritard.

(Er geginnt sich leise im Tact zu wiegen und
(he begins to sway softly to the rhythm and

mf   pp

pfeift vor sich hin,)
whistles to himself)

(gepfiffen)(whistling)

(Er wird immer lebhafter und walzt mit sei-
he becomes more and more lively and waltzes

pp

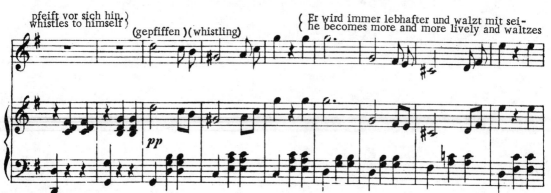

nem halbausgezogenen Paletot.)
with his overcoat, which is half off)

Tempo di marcia moderato.

besinnt sich wo er ist, sammelt sich, bemüht sich ernst zu sein und versucht von neuem den Paletot
recalling where he is, pulls himself together, tries to be serious, and tries once more to remove

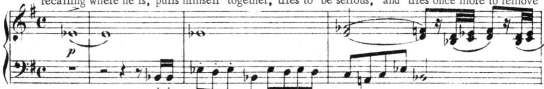

auszuziehen, was ihm endlich gelingt.)
his overcoat, which he finally succeeds in doing.)

Walzer Die gute Laune gewinnt wieder die Oberhand. Er glaubt sich im Ballsaal, macht mehrere
His good humour wins the upperhand again. He believes he is in the ballroom, he bows

Verbeugungen und lallt : "Olga, komm her; Ida auch ! Ihr gefallt mir !"Wendet sich nach der andern
several times and mumbles : "Olga, come here; Ida, too! Like you both !" He turns to the other side

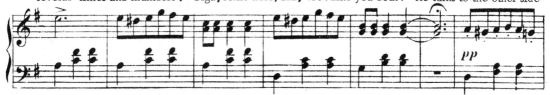

Seite und spricht mit schwerer Zunge ! " Marquis, reich mir die Hand, sei mein Freund !"
and speaks with a thick tongue ! " "Marquis, give me your hand, be my friend ! ")

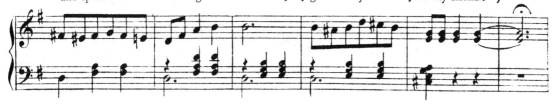

Allegretto

Singt. Angangs halblaut vor sich hin summend, - dann immer stärker)
Sings, at first humming softly to himself, then ever louder)

Die Ma-je-stät wird an-er-kannt, an-er-kannt, rings im Land;
His ma-jest-y is well-renowned, all a-round, let it ring;

jubelnd wird Champagner, der Erste sie ge-nannt! Es le-be Champagner der Er - Pst!
gai-ly we announce it;champagne is crowned the king! Long live the champagne ce-le-bra- Pst!

(Sieht sich erschrocken um, ob ihn Niemand gehört POLKA UN POCO MODERATO
(looks around, terrified, if anyone heard, and tries
und bemüht sich solid zu erscheinen (Er erblickt das Theezeug auf dem
to appear respectable) (His eye falls on the tea-things, on

rückwärtigen Tische, das kommt ihm gelegen; er trägt es schwankend und mit grosser Mühe auf den
the table upstage, which seem most opportune;he carries them, staggering and with great pains,

vorderen Tisch, zündet nach ein'gen komischen Versuchen die Spirituslampe an;es ist ihm sehr warm:
to the downstage table, and lights, after several comical attempts, the spirit lamp: he seems very

Er fachelt sich Luft und trinkt ein Glas Wasser.)
warm: he fans himself and drinks a glass of water.)

(Sinkt ermüdet in den Stuhl, ergreift eine
(sinks exhausted into the chair, grasps a

Meno mosso.

Zeitung und versucht zu lesen, - doch seine Gedanken weilen noch beim Tanze)
newspaper and attempts to read, - but his thoughts still remain on the dance.)

Walzer, piu moderato.

(Frank pfeift einschlummernd)
(Frank whistles, falling asleep)

(lässt die Zeitung sinken)
(lets the newspaper fall)

(gepfiffen)
(whistling)

(und schläft ein)
(and he sleeps)

Più lento.

156

FROSCH(erblickt Frank schlafend, für sich). Ah, der
Herr Direktor ist schon da! Er scheint sehr ver-
tieft in seine Lektüre.(Bemüht sich, stramme
Haltung anzunehmen).Ich muss ihm meinen
Rapport machen.(Sehr laut). Herr Direktor, ich
komm zum Rapport!
FRANK(fährt auf). Was gibt's? Nun, Frosch, quake
deinen Rapport!Komm näher!
FROSCH(verlegen, da er sich nicht zu rühren wagt).
Näher soll ich kommen?
FRANK.Nun freilich!(Frosch macht zwei wankende
Schritte, für sich)Der verdammte Champagner!
Alles hüpft mir vor den Augen.Auch der Frosch
hüpft!(laut). Was gibt's Neues?
FROSCH.Nichts, Herr Direktor. Nur numero 12 ver-
langt einen Advokaten.
FRANK. Der Herr von Eisenstein? Meinetwegen, das
ist sein gutes Recht.
FROSCH. Ich habe ihm einen gewissen Dr.Blind be-
stellt, den man mir anempfohlen.(Taumelt
etwas). Verdammter Slibowitz!
FRANK. Warum schwankst du denn so?
FROSCH.(immer schwankend).Ich schwanke ja nicht!
FRANK(für sich). Verfluchter Champagner! Alles
schwankt mir vor den Augen.
FROSCH(hat einen Stuhl als Halt gefunden)Sehen Sie,
Herr Direktor, ich schwanke nicht!
FRANK(heftig). Wer sagt denn, dass du schwankst?
(für sich). Verfluchte Geschichte!
FROSCH.Niemand, Herr Direktor, niemand sagt es.
(für sich). Mir kam es so vor, als ob er's ge-
sagt hätte!
FRANK.Nun, wie gefällt es dir in diesem Hause?
FROSCH(stützt sich mit beiden Armen auf Franks
Tisch). Wie es mir hier gefällt?Sehr gut!Recht
fidel ist es! Wahrhaftig, ein so fideles Gefängnis ist mir noch gar nicht vorgekommen. Meinen Sie nicht auch, Herr Direktor?
FRANK. Ja, du hast recht; sehr fidel ist's hier! (Es
läutet). Was gibt's? Man läutet an der Tür.

'ROSCH.(bleibt ruhig stehen). Ja, mir war's auch so!
FRANK.Schau aus dem Fenster, wer da ist.(Es läutet
wieder.)
FROGG.Aus dem Fenster?(für sich)Bis dorthin komm
ich ja gar nicht!(Schwankt im Zickzack zum
Fenster.)
FRANK.(für sich) Nur kein Besuch jetzt!
FROGG(am Fenster).Zwei Damen sind da!
FRANK.(aufspringend).Zwei Damen, sagst du?
FROGG. Vielleicht ist es auch nur eine.Ich sehe
alles doppelt. - Soll ich öffnen?
FRANK. Nein...ja...das heisst... nein!
FROGG.Es sind zwei hübsche feine Damen!
FRANK.So öffne doch!Warum öffnest du denn
nicht?
FROGG.Ich gehe ja schon! (Im Abgehen)Eine lust-
ige Geschichte!Zwei schöne junge Damen schon
in aller Früh! Ich sag's ja, ein fideles Gefäng-
nis! Ungeheuer fidel! (Torkelt ab.)
FRANK.Wenn ich nur schnell etwas Niederschlagendes
...(entdeckt auf dem Tisch die Wasserflasche,
schenkt sich ein Glas ein, stürzt es hinunter.)
Ah, das tut gut!(Taucht sein Taschentuch ein
und befeuchtet sich die Stirn.)
FROSCH.Die beiden Damen wollen den Herrn Chevalier Chargrin sprechen.
FRANK.(zuckt zusammen).Chevalier Chargrin!?

FROSCH.Ich habe Ihnen schon gesagt, dass wir keinen
Herrn dieses Namens hier haben.
ADELE. Aber da ist er ja!

FROGG(noticing Frank sleeping, to himself). Ah, the
director is already here. He seems immersed
in his reading.(Pulls himself together, attempt-
ing a military posture) I must make my report
to him.(very loud)Director, I've come to report!
FRANK.(leaping up)What happened? Oh, yes, Frogg,
croak out your report! Come closer!
FROGG.(confused, not daring to move)Should I come
closer?
FRANK.Certainly!(Frogg takes two wavering steps)
(to himself) That accursed champagne!Every-
thing jumps around in front of my eyes. Even
the Frogg is hopping!(aloud)What's new?
FROGG. Nothing, director.Only that number 12 is
asking for a lawyer.
FRANK.Von Eisenstein? That's right, he's got that
coming to him.
FROGG. I called the famous Dr.Blind;somebody re-
commended him for something.(swaying some-
what)Accursed liquor!
FRANK. Why are you swaying back and forth that way?
FROGG.(still swaying).I'm not swaying now!
FRANK.(to himself).Accursed champagne!Everything
seems to be swaying!
FROGG.(has found a stool to hold onto). See, director,
I'm not swaying!
FRANK.(violently). Who said you were swaying?(to
himself) Accursed position to be in!
FROGG.Nobody, director, nobody said so. (to himself)
It seemed to me he said it.

FRANK. Well, Frogg, how do you like it here?
FROGG.(leaning both elbows on Frank's desk) How do
I like it? Very well! It's very jolly! As a matter
of fact, I've never been in such a jolly jail!Don't
you think so, director?

FRANK. Yes, you have a point; it is a jolly jail!(the
bell rings)What's that? I heard some one ring, at
the door.

FROGG.(stands, without moving). Yes, I thought so, too!
FRANK. Look out the window and see who it is. (It
rings again.)
FROGG.Out the window?(to himself) I'll never get that
far!(staggers in a zig-zag towards the window)

FRANK.(to himself).Don't let it be visitors, now!
FROGG.(at the window).Two ladies are there!
FRANK.(jumping up).Two ladies, you say?
FROGG. Maybe it's only one. I might be seeing double.
Shall I open up?
FRANK. No... yes... I mean... no!
FROGG. They are two very pretty ladies!
FRANK. Then open up! Why don't you open the door?

FROGG. I'm going already!(while exiting)What a pleasant situation!Two beautiful girls arriving already,
before breakfast! I must say, it is a jolly jail!
Jumping jolly! (stumbles off)
FRANK.If I could only get something down quickly...
(discovers the carafe of water, pours himself a
glass, and gulps it down) Ah, that did me good!
(dips his handkerchief, and dampens his forehead).

FROGG. These ladies want to speak to Chevalier Chargrin.
FRANK.(startled).Chevalier Chargrin?!(pulling himself together)
FROGG. I already told them we have no one by that
name here.
ADELE. But there he is, right there!

IDA. Dr. Falke hat uns die Wohnung ganz richtig beschrieben.

FRANK(für sich).Die Olga mit der Ida,das fehlte noch!(zu Frosch).Lass uns allein!

FROSCH. Zu Befehl!(Im Abgehen).Ein lustiges Gefängnis hier! Ungeheuer fidel!

ADELE.Der Herr Chevalier wundern sich gewiss über diesen Besuch?

FRANK.Allerdings...ich hatte nicht gehofft,so früh schon...

ADELE. Wir haben Ihnen eine Bitte vorzutragen.

IDA. Und meine Schwester meinte, frisch gewagt ist halb gewonnen.Da der Herr Chevalier sich heute ganz besonders für meine Schwester zu interessieren schienen....

FRANK(verlegen).Allerdings!(für sich).Sie sind übrigens alle beide allerliebst!

ADELE. Da hielt ich es für meine Pflicht,Ihnen ein Geständnis zu machen!

FRANK. Oho!(für sich)Mir wird ganz heiss!

ADELE. Dass ich nicht das bin,was ich scheine!

FRANK.Sie sind ganz allerliebst,und das genügt mir, mein Engel!

IDA.Meine Schwester ist aber keine Künstlerin.

FRANK.(galant). Was nicht ist,kann noch werden!

ADELE.Das meinte meine Schwester auch,und deswegen kommen wir zu Ihnen.

IDA. Sie sind ein vornehmer Herr und könnten ihr leicht behilflich sein.

FRANK. Ich! Wieso?

IDA.Wie gesagt,meine Schwester ist noch nicht Künstlerin....

ADELE.Auch noch nicht einmal Elevin, sondern bis jetzt nur Stubenmädchen des Herrn von Eisenstein.

FRANK.Ein Stubenmädchen!Und Sie haben sich von mir die Hand küssen lassen?

ADELE. Den Mund ja auch!

FRANK. Pst,nichts ausplaudern!

ADELE. Es bleibt unter uns! Aber da Sie Herrn von Eisenstein sprechen werden,hätte ich noch eine Bitte.

FRANK. Nun?

ADELE. Der Herr weiss,dass ich ohne Erlaubnis der gnädigen Frau in ihrem Kleide die Villa Orlofsky besucht habe.(schluchzend) Ich bitte, ich beschwöre Sie,legen Sie ein gutes Wort für mich ein!

FRANK. Dass er Ihnen verzeiht?

ADELE. Nein,dass er mir das Kleid schenkt,weil es mir so gut steht!

FRANK.Das ist doch ein bisschen viel verlangt! Augenblicklich entlassen wird Sie Ihre Herrschaft.

IDA. Ach,wenn es weiter nichts ist,entlassen hat sie sich schon selbst.

ADELE. Ich habe nämlich die Idee,mich fürs Theater ausbilden zu lassen.

IDA. Und da sollten uns der Herr Chevalier behilflich sein. Mich hat auch so ein vornehmer Herr ausbilden lassen.

FRANK. Ich soll Sie ausbilden lassen? Ja,haben Sie denn auch Talent?

ADELE. Ob ich Talent habe? Sonderbare Frage!

IDA. Dr. Falke described the house perfectly!

FRANK(to himself).Olga with Ida,that is all I need! (to Frogg). Leave us alone!

FROGG. At your service!(as he goes off) A pleasant prison.Jollier and jollier!

ADELE.You must be wondering about our visit,Chevalier?

FRANK. As a matter of fact...I never hoped,so soon...

ADELE.We have something to ask you.

IDA. And my sister said,nothing ventured,nothing gained.As you seemed to take a special interest in my sister last night....

FRANK.(in confusion) Indeed!(to himself) I found them both very lovable!

ADELE. So I felt it was my duty to make a confession to you!

FRANK. Hoho(to himself) It's getting very warm!

ADELE. That I am not what I seem to be!

FRANK.You are completely enchanting,and that is enough for me,my angel!

IDA. But my sister isn't really an actress.

FRANK.(gallant) What is not, could well come to be!

ADELE. That's just what my sister says,and that's why I came to you!

IDA. You are such a noble gentleman,and maybe you could help her!

FRANK. I? In what way?

IDA. Well,as we said,my sister is not an actress yet...

ADELE.Not even a beginner,so far I'm just the chambermaid at the Eisenstein house.

FRANK. A chambermaid!And you let me kiss your hand?

ADELE. My lips,too!

FRANK. Psst,don't mention that!

ADELE. It will be our secret! But since you will be speaking to Mr. von Eisenstein,I have a favour to ask you.

FRANK. Well?

ADELE. He knows I wore my mistress' dress to the Villa Orlofsky,without her permission.(sobbing) I beg you, I implore you, to put in a word for me.

FRANK. So he'll forgive you?

ADELE. Oh,no,so he'll let me keep the dress,since it is so becoming!

FRANK. That is a little too much to expect! They will let you go on the spot!

IDA. Ah,if that's the only thing,she has already let herself go!

ADELE. Because I had an idea I could let myself be developed for the theatre!

IDA. And that is where you come in,Chevalier. I let just such a fine gentleman develop me!

FRANK. I should have you developed? Yes,but have you any talent?

ADELE. Have I got talent? What a question!

Nº 14 . COUPLETS.

No. 14 COUPLETS

160

Meno mosso.

das gesehn, müssen Sie ge-stehn, es wär' der Scha-den nicht ge-ring, wenn mit
you can see, sure-ly you a-gree, to waste such tal-ent is all wrong, with so

dem Ta-lent, mit dem Ta-lent ich nicht zum The-a-ter ging!
much to show, so much to show, the stage is where I be-long!

Tempo di marcia.

Spiel' ich ei-ne Kö-ni-gin schreit'
How well I could play a queen, Her

ich ma-je-stä-tisch hin, ni-cke hier und ni-cke da, ja
ma-jes-ty so se-rene, bow-ing there, and nod-ding here, in

ganz, ach, in mei-ner Glo-ri-a! Al-les macht voll
all, ah, my glo-ry I'll ap-pear! Courtiers pay-ing

162

durch geb' ich nicht nach, doch ach, im drit-ten werd' ich schwach: da öff-net plötz-lich sich die
acts, I will not sin, but in the third, at last, give in: when all at once, in-to the

Thür; o weh, mein Mann, was wird aus mir, ach!
room, my hus-band bursts; it is my doom, ah!

lento a piacere

Ver-zei-hung, flöt'ich, er ver-zeiht; ach,
But he for-gives me and with-draws, ah,

ad lib.

zum Schluss Tab-leau, da wei-nen d'Leut; ach, ach,
the cur-tain falls to great ap-plause, ah, ah,

colla parte

Più mosso.

ja!
yes!

FRANK(spricht) Zum Stubenmädchen sind Sie allerdings etwas emanzipiert!
IDA. Sie wollen also meine Schwester ausbilden lassen,Herr Chevalier?
    (Es läutet.)
FRANK.(ans Fenster gehend).Ich muss doch sehen, wer da ist?(prallt erschrocken zurück.)Donnerwetter,Marquis Renard! Was mach ich nun?
FROSCH(ist gekommen).Soll ich öffnen?
FRANK. Ja... nein...warte noch!(für sich)Ich bin ganz konfus!(zu Frosch)Führe die Damen in ein anderes Zimmer!
FROSCH.Ich habe nur noch Numero 13 frei!
FRANK.So führe sie auf Nummer 13!
    (Es leütet wieder)
FROSCH.(leise) So werden sie also eingesperrt?
FRANK.Nein...das heisst ja!Meinetwegen!Sperre sie ein,mach nur,dass sie fortkommen!Was mag der Marquis hier wollen?
FROSCH.Wollen Sie die Güte haben,meine Damen?
ADELE. Ist Numero 13 Ihr Empfangssalon?
FROSCH. Freilich!Oh,wir haben mehrere solche Salons,weil wir oft längeren Besuch bekommen.
IDA. Also führen Sie uns auf Nummer 13!
FROSCH.(beiden Damen den Arm bietend).Wenn's gefällig?(Adele und Ida hängen sich ein.) Fideles Gefängnis bei uns! Ungeheuer fidel!
    (Ab mit Adele und Ida)
FRANK(allein).Der Herr Marquis Renard wird schon ungeduldig. Was soll ich machen? Ich muss ihn hereinlassen auf die Gefahr hin,dass die Sache mit einer ungeheuren Blamage für mich endet. (Öffnet die Tür.)
EISENSTEIN.(tritt ein).Ist's möglich,teurer Chevalier,dich find ich hier?Bist du wegen nächtlicher Ruhestörung arretiert worden?
FRANK.Erst sag mir,lieber Marquis,was du hier zu tun hast?
EISENSTEIN.Ah,du bist beim Tee,das kommt mir sehr apropos.Du erlaubst schon!(setzt sich).
FRANK.Bitte,bediene dich ungeniert. Tu,als ob du zu Hause wärst!
EISENSTEIN. Das bin ich eigentlich jetzt auch!
FRANK.Du hier zu Hause? Das könnte ich doch wohl eher von mir behaupten.
EISENSTEIN.So sag mir doch endlich,was hast du denn getrieben,dass du hier eingesperrt wurdest, Chevalier?
FRANK.Ich bin ja gar nicht eingesperrt!
EISENSTEIN.Zum Henker,was machst du dann aber hier?
FRANK.So hör denn,ich muss endlich die Wahrheit bekennen: ich bin nicht der Chevalier Chargrin,sondern heisse Frank und bin Direktor dieses Gefängnisses!
EISENSTEIN.Haha,ein guter Spass! Ein prächtiger Spass,haha!
FRANK.Kein Spass,sondern bitterer Ernst!
EISENSTEIN.Mein Gott,Chevalier,bist du denn noch so arg betrunken,dass du dir wirklich einbildest, hier Gefängnisdirektor zu sein?Nimm noch eine Tasse Tee!
FRANK.Keiner mehr da :Kein Tee,kein Chevalier!
EISENSTEIN.Geh,Bruder,geh ;du willst mich zum besten haben!
FRANK.Du zweifelst daran?(läutet.)Sollst dich gleich überzeugen!

FROSCH.Herr Diektor befehlen?
FRANK. Pack den Harrn Marquis!
FROSCH.Sehr wohl! - Soll ich ihm Handschellen anlegen? (Packt Eisenstein.)
EISENSTEIN. Was soll das heissen?
FRANK. Lass ihn wieder los! Es war nur ein Spass.

FRANK.You certainly seem much too well-developed already for a chambermaid!
IDA. Will you help my sister develop her talent,Chevalier?
    (the bell rings)
FRANK.(going to the window) I must see who that is. (taken aback,in shock) Good Lord in Heaven, Marquis Renard! What'll I do now?
FROGG.(having entered) Should I open the door?
FRANK. Yes... no... not yet(to himself) Now I'm completely confused! (to Frogg) Show the ladies into another room!
FROGG. Number 13 is the only one free!
FRANK.Then show them to number 13!
    (the bell rings again)
FROGG.(softly)So they're to be locked up,too?
FRANK. No!That is,yes!It's all the same! Lock them up,but just get them out of here!What could the Marquis want here?
FROGG. Would you be so kind,ladies?
ADELE. Is number 13 your reception room?
FROGG.Definitely! Oh,we have quite a few rooms of that type,since some of our visitors do,that is, spend a lot of time.
IDA. Well,then,lead on, to number 13!
FROGG.(offering an arm to each lady)Whenever you're ready?(Adele and Ida take his arms)Jolly jail! Jolly,jolly,jolly! (exits with Ida and Adele)
FRANK(alone).Marquis Renard must be getting impatient.What shall I do? I'll have to receive him,even at the risk of making myself a terrible laughing stock over the whole affair.(opens the door.)
EISENSTEIN.(enters).Can it be possible,my dear Chevalier,to find you here?Did they arrest you for disturbing the peace?
FRANK.Tell me first,my dear Marquis,what are you doing here?
EISENSTEIN.Ah,you're just having tea,what a splendid idea!With your permission!(sits down)
FRANK.Please help yourself!Make yourself at home!

EISENSTEIN.Well,one might say I am at home,now!
FRANK. You're at home,here? I could better say that about myself.
EISENSTEIN.So,no,tell me at last,what did you do to get arrested,Chevalier?

FRANK.I haven't been arrested!
EISENSTEIN.The devil,what are you doing here,then?

FRANK.Well,if you'll listen a moment,I'll have to tell you the truth. I am not the Chevalier Chargrin; my name is Frank,and I'm the director of this prison!
EISENSTEIN.Haha, that's wonderful! You're a better practical joker than even I am!
FRANK.It's no joke,I'm afraid it's the bitter truth!
EISENSTEIN.Good Lord,Chevalier,you can't be so drunk that you've got delusions about being a prison director... can you? Here, have some more tea!
FRANK.There is no more :no more tea,no more Chevalier!
EISENSTEIN.Go on,brother,go on!You do want to get the best of me!
FRANK. You doubt my word?(rings)You shall soon be convinced!
FROGG. You rang, Director?
FRANK. Arrest the Marquis!
FROGG.Yes,sir! Shall I put him in handcuffs? (holds Eisenstein).
EISENSTEIN.What's the meaning of this?
FRANK. Let him go again!It was only a little joke.

FROSCH. (lässt los). Ah so, nur ein Spass!

FRANK. Geh und lass uns jetzt allein!

FROSCH. Kuriose Spässe! Ich sag's ja, ein fideles Gefängnis, ungeheuer fidel! (ab.)

FRANK. Bist du nun endlich überzeugt?

EISENSTEIN. Allerdings, nach so handgreiflicher Beweisführung....

FRANK. Du wirst mir nicht böse sein, Marquis, dass ich ein so drastisches Mittel anwendete.

EISENSTEIN. Ich kann dir um so weniger böse sein, als du vollkommen das Recht hättest, mich einkasteln zu lassen.

FRANK. Was willst du damit sagen, Bruder Marquis?

EISENSTEIN. Vor allem lass mich mit deinen Marquis zufrieden. Ich bin kein Marquis.

FRANK. Du scherzest!

EISENSTEIN. Ich bin ebensowenig Marquis Renard wie du Chevalier Chargrin bist!

FRANK. Was sagst du?

EISENSTEIN. Ich heisse Eisenstein und komme, meine achttägige Arreststrafe abzubüssen. Sei also so gut, Bruder Gefängnisdirektor, mir meine Chambre séparée anzuweisen.

FRANK. Haha, der Witz ist nicht schlecht ausgedacht!

EISENSTEIN. Wieso Witz?

FRANK. Du willst mir mit gleicher Münze dienen. Aber unglücklicherweise geht die Geschichte nicht.

EISENSTEIN. Was heisst das?

FRANK. Das heisst, wie ich dir bewiesen habe, dass ich Gefängnisdirektor bin, kann ich dir auch beweisen dass du nicht Eisenstein bist!

EISENSTEIN. Ich bin nicht Eisenstein? Auf den Beweis wäre ich doch neugierig!

FRANK. Nun denn, ich habe Eisenstein gestern abend persönlich arretiert!

EISENSTEIN. Du hast ihn arretiert! Wo und wann?

FRANK. Gestern abend zehn Uhr in seiner Wohnung.

EISENSTEIN. War er denn zu Hause?

FRANK. Natürlich, er sass ganz gemütlich im Schlafrock mit seiner Frau beim Souper.

EISENSTEIN. (erregt). Im Schlafrock? Mit seiner Frau?

FRANK. Sie nahmen so zärtlichen Abschied, dass ich ganz gerührt wurde.

EISENSTEIN. Zärtlichen Abschied? Im Schlafrock! Nein, nein, das ist unmöglich! Und wo... wo ist dieser Herr Von Eisenstein jetzt?

FRANK. Er sitzt auf Numero 12!

EISENSTEIN. Auf Numero 12? Ich muss ihn sogleich sehen!

FRANK. Es tut mir leid, aber ohne Erlaubnisschein darf niemand zu den Gefangenen.

FROSCH. Immer fideler wird's bei uns in Gefängnis! Jetzt ist schon wieder eine da!

FRANK. Was willst du?

FROSCH. Es ist wieder eine Dame.

FRANK. Was sagst du? Eine Dame?

FROSCH. Jawohl, eine Dame! 's ist ja nicht die erste heut!

FRANK. Wie sieht sie aus?

FROSCH. Sie ist zwar verschleiert, aber aus ihrem Gehaben schliesse ich, dass sie hübsch ist. Ich habe sie ins Sprechzimmer geführt.

FRANK. Eine verschleierte Dame? (zu Eisenstein, der vor sich hinbrütet). Du entschuldigst mich einen Augenblick. (Ab.)

FROGG. (lets go) Ah, only a joke!

FRANK. You may go now and leave us alone!

FROGG. Funny jokes! I say it again, this certainly is a jolly jail, mighty jolly! (exits)

FRANK. Are you finally convinced?

EISENSTEIN. Indeed, after such violently physical proof....

FRANK. You won't be angry with me, Marquis, that I was forced to take such drastic measures?

EISENSTEIN. I can't very well be angry with you, when you have the perfect right to have me arrested.

FRANK. What do you mean by that, brother Marquis?

EISENSTEIN. First, you can forget the Marquis business. I'm no Marquis.

FRANK. You're joking!

EISENSTEIN. I'm exactly as much Marquis Renard as you are Chevalier Chargrin!

FRANK. What are you saying?

EISENSTEIN. My name is Eisenstein, and I've come to start my eight days' sentence in jail. If you will be so kind, Mr. Director, as to show me to my private suite!

FRANK. Haha, that's not bad! That's quite a witty joke!

EISENSTEIN. What's witty?

FRANK. You'd like to pay me back in my own coin. But unfortunately, it won't work.

EISENSTEIN. What do you mean?

FRANK. I mean, that just as I proved to you that I am the prison director, so I can easily prove that you are not Eisenstein!

EISENSTEIN. I am not Eisenstein? Well, I'm really curious as to how you can prove that!

FRANK. Well, then, last night, I personally arrested Eisenstein!

EISENSTEIN. You arrested him? Where and when?

FRANK. Last night, about ten o'clock, in his house.

EISENSTEIN. He was in his house then?

FRANK. Of course, he was sitting very cozily in his dressing gown, having supper with his wife.

EISENSTEIN. (excited) In his dressing gown? With his wife?

FRANK. They took such a tender farewell, even I was touched.

EISENSTEIN. Tender farewell? In dressing-gown! No, no, that's impossible! And where... where is this Mr. Eisenstein now?

FRANK. He's sitting in Number 12!

EISENSTEIN. In number 12? I have to see him, immediately!

FRANK. I'm very sorry, but no one may see the prisoners without a permit.

FROGG. This jail gets jollier and jollier! Now there's another one there!

FRANK. What do you want?

FROGG. It's another lady.

FRANK. What did you say? A lady?

FROGG. Yes, indeed a lady! It's not the first today!

FRANK. What does she look like?

FROGG. She is veiled, but from the way she acts, she must be pretty. I left her in the waiting room.

FRANK. A veiled lady? (to Eisenstein, who is lost in meditation) You'll have to excuse me for a moment. (goes off).

FROSCH. Wenn ich die auch wieder einsperren soll, weiss ich wahrhaftig nicht, wohin. (Es läutet). Schon wieder etwas! Keinen Augenblick Ruhe hat man; aber fidel ist's heute bei uns, das muss wahr sein, ungeheuer fidel! (Ab.)

EISENSTEIN (allein). Ein anderer wurde also in meiner Wohnung arretiert und hier eingesperrt! Dieser zweite Ich hat mit meiner Frau soupiert, während ich.... Diese Entdeckung hat mich auf einmal ganz nüchtern gemacht. Ich brauche keinen Tee mehr, aber einen Erlaubnisschein brauche ich, wenn ich mich besuchen und mit mir selbst reden will! Es ist zum Tollwerden!

FROSCH (führt Blind, der wie im 1. Akt gekleidet ist, herein). Bitte, nur hier zu warten, Herr Doktor. Ich hole den Herrn von Eisenstein. (Ab.)

BLIND (erblickt Eisenstein). Was sagt der Mensch? Er holt Sie? Sie sind ja schon da!

EISENSTEIN. Das geht Sie gar nichts an! Ich bin nicht nur da, sondern auch dort! Was wollen Sie hier, rechtsverdrehender Aktenwurm?

BLIND. Was ich hier will? Sie haben mich doch rufen lassen.

EISENSTEIN. Ich hätte Sie rufen lassen?

BLIND. Aber der Amtsdiener sagte doch ausdrücklich, dass mich Herr von Eisenstein zu sich bescheiden lasse!

EISENSTEIN. Weil Herr von Eisenstein ein Dummkopf ist!

BLIND. Wohl möglich, aber....

EISENSTEIN. Das heisst, nicht ich, sondern der andere ist der Dummkopf! -Halt, eine Idee! Sie müssen mir Ihre Stelle abtreten!

BLIND. Meine Stelle? Herr von Eisenstein stehen sich doch viel besser!

EISENSTEIN. Nur bei der Zusammenkunft mit Herrn von Eisenstein; so kann ich ihn kennenlernen und ihn zugleich aufs genaueste inquirieren.

BLIND. Sie reden ja later konfuses Zeug!

EISENSTEIN. Um so mehr werde ich Ihnen gleichen! Ihren Rock brauche ich, Ihre Perücke, Brille und Akten! Vorwärts, Sie armseliger Aufklauber von Milderungsgründen, sonst erdrossle ich Sie! (treibt ihn rückwärts ab.)

FROSCH. Herr Notar Blind, hier ist der Herr von Numero 12, der Sie zu sprechen wünscht!

ALFRED. (In Eisensteins Schlafrock und Kappe). Es ist aber niemand zu sehen.

FROSCH. Das ist auch unmöglich, denn der ist ja-Blind! (für sich). Verdammter Slibowitz! (Ab.)

ALFRED. (allein) Ich muss gestehen, mein Abenteuer fängt an, mich zu langweilen. Es ist bereits Tag, und wie es scheint, kümmert sich kein Mensch um mich. Ist das der Lohn meiner Diskretion? (Rosalinde tritt herein.) Aber nein, ich bin nicht verlassen; die Himmlische kommt selbst, mich in meinem Kerker zu trösten. Fürwahr, das ist edel, das ist geradezu romantisch!

ROSALINDE. Hier ist von keiner Romantik die Rede! Hören Sie!

ALFRED. Ich höre.

ROSALINDE. Sie müssen so bald wie möglich fort von hier!

ALFRED. Ach ja, darum möchte ich auch bitten!

ROSALINDE. Mein Gatte kann jeden Augenblick hier erscheinen; er darf Sie nicht finden, am wenigsten in diesem Aufzuge!

FROGG. If I have to lock her up, too, I just don't know where I'll put her. (the bell rings) Now there's something else! Never a dull moment; it's a busy day around here, and that's the truth! But...it's jolly! (goes off.)

EISENSTEIN. (alone). Some one else was arrested in my house, and is now in this very jail! Another me had supper with my wife, while I... This discovery has sobered me up completely! I have no need for tea, now; what I need is a permit to visit myself! This is insanity!

FROGG. (with Blind, who is dressed as in Act I) Please wait here, Doctor. I'll bring in Mr. Eisenstein. (exits)

BLIND. (catching sight of Eisenstein) What did that fellow say? He'd bring you? You're already here!

EISENSTEIN. That's neither here, nor there! I'm not only here, I'm also there! What do you want here, you law-squeezing bookworm?

BLIND. What do I want here? You were the one who sent for me.

EISENSTEIN. I sent for you?

BLIND. But the office clerk told me expressly that Mr. von Eisenstein wanted me at his side!

EISENSTEIN. Because Mr. von Eisenstein is an idiot!

BLIND. Very likely, but....

EISENSTEIN. I don't mean me, the other is the idiot! Wait, an idea! You must let me take your place!

BLIND. My place? But the Eisenstein place is much better!

EISENSTEIN. Only for the appointment with Mr. von Eisenstein; so I can get to know him, and make some detailed inquiries.

BLIND. You always say the most confusing things!

EISENSTEIN. I shall resemble you all the more! I need your robe, your wig, spectacles and briefcase! Forward, march, you pitiful pusher of appeals, or I'll Strangle you! (pushes him off backwards)

FROGG. Doctor Blind, here is the gentleman from number 12, who wanted to see you.

ALFRED. (in Eisenstein's dressing-gown and night-cap) But I don't see anyone.

FROGG. That's very likely, after all he is Blind. (to himself) Accursed liquor! (exits).

ALFRED. (alone) I must admit, this adventure is beginning to bore me. It's daylight already, and not a soul appears to take any interest in me. Is that what I get for my discretion? (Rosalinda appears) Ah, no, I have not been abandoned; the divine one herself comes to console me in my dungeon. Indeed, how noble, how truly romantic!

ROSALINDA. This is no place to speak of romance! Listen to me!

ALFRED. I'm listening.

ROSALINDA. You must leave here as soon as possible!

ALFRED. Ah, yes, it had occured to me to request that myself!

ROSALINDA. Any moment now my husband may show up; he must not find you here, especially in that outfit!

ALFRED. Richtig, er könnte mir übelnehmen, dass ich seinen Schlafrock annektierte !

ROSALINDE. Er hat sich zwar unwürdig benommen, unverantwortlich....

ALFRED. Ja, unverantwortlich, dass er mich so lange schmachten liess in diesem Arreste !

ROSALINDE. Während er sich bei einem Souper des Prinzen Orlofsky amüsierte !

ALFRED. Bei meinem Prinzen ! Oh, der Schlankel !

ROSALINDE. Aber nichtsdestoweniger ist meine Lage entsetzlich, und ich weiss mir keinen Rat.

ALFRED. Vielleicht weiss der Notar Rat, den ich mir eben herholen liess.

ROSALINDE. Ein Notar !

ALFRED (zur Tür blickend). Hier ist er schon !

EISENSTEIN. (für sich). Ha, die Treulose ist bei ihm ! Jetzt Fassung und Ruhe; ich muss erfahren, wie sie miteinander stehen !

ALFRED. Quite right, he might object to my appropriating his dressing-gown !

ROSALINDA. Even though he behaved in such an unworthy, irresponsible...

ALFRED. Irresponsible indeed, to leave me languishing so long in jail !

ROSALINDA. While he was having a gay time at Prince Orlofsky's dinner !

ALFRED. At the prince's ? Oh, the rogue !

ROSALINDA. But nevertheless, my position is dreadful, and I don't know what will help me.

ALFRED. Maybe the lawyer I sent for knows something.

ROSALINDA. A lawyer?

ALFRED. (looking at the door). Here he is now !

EISENSTEIN. (to himself). Ha, the faithless one is with him! Now to be calm and composed; I must find out exactly where things stand !

Nᵒ 15. TERZETT.

No. 15   TRIO

170

ROSAL.

heh- len, in - dess ich mir No - ti - zen ma-che! Der Fall ist ei - gen-
-mit- ted; I shall take notes and solve the myst-'ry! It's all ex - ag - ger-

ALFRED.

thüm- lich, wie Sie gleich werden sehn. So gar ver-wi-ckelt ziem-lich, das muss man einge-
-a - tion, as you will sure-ly see. There is some com-pli - ca-tion, to that I must a-

EISENST.

stehn! Nun denn, so ge- ben Sie zu Pro- to - koll, wo-rin ich Sie ver-theid'- gen
-gree! Come, with your state-ment we will now com-mence. I must de - cide on your de-

soll!
-fense!

acceler.

ALFRED.

Ein
Some

Allegretto.

selt - sam A - ben - teu - er ist ge - stern mir pas - sirt: man hat mich aus Ver -
fun - ny things have happened to me, since yes - ter - day; while with this charming

se - hen hier in Ar - rest ge - führt, weil ich mit die - ser Da - me ein
la - dy I dined, a lit - tle late, I wrong - ly was ar - rest - ed, and

(erstaunt)
(astonished)

we - nig spät sou - pirt. Was
thrown in jail to wait. How

EISENST. (heftig)
(violently)

Ein Glück, dass es so kam; Sie han - del - ten in - fam!
Thank God, they were in time; so in - fam - ous a crime!

kommt denn Ihnen in den Sinn? Sie soll'n mich ja ver - theid'gen.
dare you, have you gone in - sane? You've come here to defend me.

(sich fassend)
(controlling himself)

Ver - zeih'n Sie, wenn ich
You must for - give me,

174

Recitativ.

184

186

ROSALINDE(spricht).Also du willst mir Vorwürfe machen,du willst von Treulosigkeit sprechen, nachdem ich doch ganz genau weiss(ihm seine Uhr unter die Nase haltend),wieviel es bei dir geschlagen hat!

EISENSTEIN,(verblüfft).Meine Uhr! Alle Teufel,an die dachte ich gar nicht mehr!

ROSALINDE.Wollen Sie wieder die Schläge meines Herzens zählen,Herr Marquis?

EISENST. (für sich).Sie war meine Ungarin? O ich Einfaltspinsel!

ALFRED.Also Sie sind Herr von Eisenstein?

EISENSTEIN.Ja,ich bin Eisenstein,der Besitzer dieses samtenen Weibes und dieses meineidigen Schlafrocks!

ALFRED.Ich stelle Ihnen beides mit Dank zurück.

EISENSTEIN. Sie werden mir Satisfaktion geben, und zwar sogleich!

ALFRED.Sogleich?Unmöglich!Erst werden Sie die Güte haben,sich in die Zelle Numero 12 zu begeben,deren legitimer Besitzer Sie gleichfalls sind!

ROSALINDE. Was sagen Sie?

ALFRED.Ich sage,dass Ihr Herr Gemahl seine übrigen sieben Tage absitzen soll;ich habe an dem einen genug!

FALKE.Ah,wie ich sehe,hat's hier schon eine Erkennungsszene gegeben!

ROSALINDE.Doktor,was haben Sie angestellt?

ALFRED.Allerdings,der wahre Herr von Eisenstein hat sich dekuvriert und brennt vor Verlangen, den vor mir unrechtmässig okkupierten Platz in seiner Zelle einzunehmen.

EISENSTEIN.Niemals! Ich bin nicht Herr von Eisenstein! Wer will mir beweisen,dass ich Eisenstein bin? Ins Gefängnis - nimmermehr!

FRANK. Es sollte mir leid tun,wenn ich gegen meinen Duzbruder und Landsmann Gewaltmittel anwenden müsste!

FROSCH.Herr Direktor,die beiden Damen auf Numero 13 machen einen Mordsspektakel.

FRANK. Ach,die hatte ich vergessen!Lass sie heraus und führe sie hierher!

FROSCH(im Abgehn).Fideles Gefängnis!

ROSALINDE.Wer sind die beiden Damen?

FRANK.Keine Unbekannten,gnädige Frau. Die eine besonders kennen Sie gut!

ADELE.(aufgeregt herein).Abscheulich!

IDA.(hinter ihr).Schändlich!

ADELE.(zu Frank).Wie,mein Herr,Sie lassen mich und meine Schwester in ein Gefängnis sperren?

IDA. Was haben wir denn verbrochen?

FRANK.Ich bitte um Entschuldigung.Ein Versehen dieses Menschen!(deutet auf Frosch).

FROSCH.Aber der Herr Gefängnisdirektor sagten ja...

ADELE.Gefängnisdirektor?

FRANK.Allerdings,und als solcher frage ich Sie (deutet auf Eisenstein),kennen Sie diesen Herrn?

ADELE.Herr von Eisenstein und meine verflossene Gnädige!

EISENSTEIN.Was kümmert mich dieses Zeugnis? Ich gehe nun einmal nicht ins Gefängnis!

FALKE. Nun,dann müssen wir noch weitere Zeugen kommen lassen!(Öffnet die Mitteltür).

FROSCH. Noch mehr? 's wird immer fideler bei uns.

ROSALINDA.(speaking).You think you can reproach me and carry on about infidelity,while I know all too well(thrusting his watch in front of his nose)what time it is!

EISENSTEIN.(taken aback).My watch! The devil take it, I'd forgotten all about that!

ROSALINDA. Would you care to count the beating of my heart again,Marquis?

EISENSTEIN.(to himself).She was my Hungarian countess? Oh,what a fool I've made of myself!

ALFRED. Then you must be Mr.von Eisenstein?

EISENSTEIN. Yes,I am Eisenstein,the owner of this entire woman as well as that unfaithful dressing-gown!

ALFRED. I return them both to you,most gratefully.

EISENSTEIN.You will give me satisfaction,and immediately!

ALFRED. Immediately? Impossible!First you must be kind enough to accept also your position in cell number 12,of which you are also the legitimate owner!

ROSALINDA. Whar are you saying?

ALFRED. I said,your husband can sit out his remaining seven days;one was enough for me!

FALKE. Ah,I see we've already had our scene of reunion!

ROSALINDA. Doctor,what have you done?

ALFRED.Indeed,the real Mr. von Eisenstein has discovered himself,and is burning to take his proper place,which I so unjustly occupied,in his cell!

EISENSTEIN. Never!I am not Eisenstein!Who will prove that I am von Eisenstein? Go to prison - not on your life!

FRANK. I should be very sorry to have to use force against my brother and compatriot!

FROGG.Direktor,the two ladies in number 13 are shouting bloody murder!

FRANK. Ah,I'd almost forgotten them! Let them out, and show them in here!

FROGG.(in leaving).Jolly jail!

ROSALINDA. Who are the two ladies?

FRANK.They are not unknowns,my lady. One of them, you know especially well!

ADELE.(entering,excitedly). Infamous!

IDA. (behind her). Shameful!

ADELE. (to Frank). Sir,how could you let my sister and me be put in prison?

IDA. What have we done?

FRANK. I beg your forgiveness.A little misunderstanding by this fellow!(pointing at Frogg).

FROGG. But the prison director said....

ADELE. Prison director?

FRANK. To be sure,and as such,I ask you,(pointing to Eisenstein)Do you know this gentleman?

ADELE.Mr. von Eisenstein and my one-time mistress!

EISENSTEIN.What do I care for her testimony? I am absolutely not going to jail,now!

FALKE. Well,then,we'll have to look for more witnesses! (opens the center door)

FROGG. Still more? It gets jollier every minute around here!

№ 16. FINALE III.

Rosalinde, Adele.

Ida, Orlofsky.

Eisenstein.

Frank, Falke.

Melanie, Faustine, Felicita, Minnie, Hermine, Sabine u. S o p r a n i.
and Sopranos

Ramusin, Ali Bey u. T e n o r i.
and Tenors

Murray, Cariconi u. B a s s i.
and Basses

PIANO.

O Fle-der-maus, o Fle-der-maus, lass end-lich jetzt dein O-pfer aus; der
The vengeance of the bat is won, now let the vic-tim share the fun; you've

O Fle-der-maus, o Fle-der-maus, lass end-lich jetzt dein O-pfer aus; der
The vengeance of the bat is won, now let the vic-tim share the fun; you've

FRANK.

O Fle-der-maus, o Fle-der-maus, lass end-lich jetzt dein O-pfer aus; der
The vengeance of the bat is won, now let the vic-tim share the fun; you've

O Fle-der-maus, o Fle-der-maus, lass end-lich jetzt dein O-pfer aus; der
The vengeance of the bat is won, now let the vic-tim share the fun; you've

O Fle-der-maus, o Fle-der-maus, lass end-lich jetzt dein O-pfer aus; der
The vengeance of the bat is won, now let the vic-tim share the fun; you've

O Fle-der-maus, o Fle-der-maus, lass end-lich jetzt dein O-pfer aus; der
The vengeance of the bat is won, now let the vic-tim share the fun; you've

190

Fle - der-maus, o Fle-der-maus, lass end-lich jetzt dein O-pfer aus; der ar - me Mann, der
ven-geance of the bat is won, we'll let the vic - tim share the fun; you've got the best of

Fle - der-maus, o Fle-der-maus, lass end-lich jetzt dein O-pfer aus; der ar - me Mann, der
ven-geance of the bat is won, we'll let the vic - tim share the fun; you've got the best of

Fle - der-maus, o Fle-der-maus, lass end-lich jetzt dein O-pfer aus; der ar - me Mann, der
ven-geance of the bat is won, we'll let the vic - tim share the fun; you've got the best of

ar - me Mann ist gar zu ü - bel dran!
him to - night, he is a sor - ry sight!

ar - me Mann ist gar zu ü - bel dran!
him to - night, he is a sor - ry sight!

ar - me Mann ist gar zu ü - bel dran!
him to - night, he is a sor - ry sight!

EISENST.

So er-klärt mir
Do not keep me

FALKE.

doch, ich bitt'! Al - les, was Dir sor - gen macht, war ein Scherz von mir er -
in sus - pense! All this wild co - in - ci - dence was my joke, at your ex -

ROS.ADELE.ORL.

Più mosso.

er-ste ge-nannt!,
cham-pagne is the king!

Er -ste ge-nannt!
-pagne is crowned king!

Er - ste ge-nannt!
-pagne is crowned king!

Er - ste ge-nannt!
-pagne is crowned king!

Piu mosso.

Ende der Operette
End of the Operetta